Managing Change

Roger Plant is a consultant. He was, until recently, Client Director at Ashridge Management College where he is now an Associate. He was OD advisor in Shell International, South East Asian Region, prior to that and has also worked as Personnel Manager in the engineering industry. He consults and teaches in the areas of change management, corporate culture and associated behavioural skills such as team development. He also runs, for Ashridge, a series of Action Learning Groups for Chief Executives.

Other titles for The Successful Manager

Managing Your Own Career, Dave Francis
Manage Your Time, Sally Garratt
Superteams, Colin Hastings, Peter Bixby, Rani Chaudhry-Lawton
The Roots of Excellence, Ronnie Lessem
Managing Yourself, Mike Pedler and Tom Boydell
Finance for the Perplexed Executive, Ray Proctor

Roger Plant

Managing Change
and Making It Stick

Fontana/Collins

First published in 1987 by Fontana Paperbacks
8 Grafton Street, London W1X 3LA

Set in Linotron Times
Made and printed in Great Britain by
William Collins Sons & Co. Ltd, Glasgow

Contents

Acknowledgements   7
Preface   9

Introduction   11

SECTION 1 **How do we get there?**
          Planning for implementability of change   17

Why does resistance exist?   18
How to make change happen   20
How to reduce resistance   22
The six key activities for
   successful implementation   32

SECTION 2 **Change starts with you**   37

Learning and change   37
Reflection and analysis   39
Vision and concept-building   39
Action   39
What power do you have and how
   do you use it?   40
The power of role   44
Ten dimensions of role effectiveness   45
Role effectiveness profile: a
   tool for self-assessment   50
Exerting influence – the styles you use   56

SECTION 3 **Recognizing the need and mobilizing the commitment
            to change** 62

Conditions for effective recognition 64
Mobilizing commitment 66

SECTION 4 **Where do we want to get to?**
            Building a vision for change 73

Creating a vision of the future – a case study 74

SECTION 5 **Where are we now?** 87

Stages of organizational development 87
The five phases of growth and crisis 91
The management of crisis 94
An open systems view of organizations 95
Organizational profile: a tool for assessment 103
Three phases of development 111
The principles of development 124
Applying the developmental approach 126
Where are we now? A process view 128
Diagnosing readiness to change 145

Select Bibliography 151

Acknowledgements

I want to thank those friends in many organizations who have given me their valuable time and allowed me to draw on their experience – in particular Anz Grindlays Bank, TSB, British Telecom, Mercantile & General Reinsurance, Ciba-Geigy, Willis Faber.

Special thanks must go to Maureen Edgar, Miriam Tassell and Liz Tabel for the typing, and seemingly endless retyping, of the manuscript, to Ken Walker for the illustrations and Ashridge Management College for the time to write it.

Finally to my wife Joan who kept me going and helped to make it happen.

Preface

Writing this book has been rather like a change process in an organization. The awareness and the concept have been there for a long time but somehow day-to-day affairs kept getting in the way. There was never quite enough energy mobilized to make it happen – until I allowed myself to get committed to a deadline and a contract It became an objective and then it became real for the first time. Then the panic really set in! Somehow, talking about writing a book – just like talking about change – is quite comfortable. Doing it is hard work and requires a lot of friends, support and persistence – as does making changes happen.

I am very clear about what this book is not. It is not a quick recipe for 'how to be successful at excellent changing', nor is it a deeply researched, academic thesis on change. It is really a compendium of experience and ideas. The experience is mine, the ideas are a mixture of mine and hundreds of others. Where the sources of the ideas are known, and clear, I will make reference to them. Mostly they are my own variations of and adaptations from many sources.

I want to use my own experiences of thinking about, working with, succeeding and failing to implement changes as a vehicle for provoking thought amongst you in organizations who are involved in managing changes. If it causes you to stop and think, ask a few searching questions (or see ways forward you hadn't considered before), it has done what I hoped for.

There are no answers, but there are a lot of good questions. Getting better at steering our way through the organization sea and making changes stick is all about asking good questions of the right people.

As Reg Revans puts it so succinctly when talking about his Action Learning Projects, 'We have to have experts to find answers to the difficult questions but what I'm interested in is who is going to ask the right bloody questions?'

I hope this book will go some way towards helping you ask the right questions when you haven't a clue what to do next.

Broadly I have chosen to view the bringing about of change as a five-stage process. The divisions are artificial in reality but helpful for discussion.

1. Recognizing the need to change.
2. Mobilizing commitment of the critical mass.
3. Building a shared vision.
4. Diagnosing current reality.
5. Getting there.

This is the logical order in which the book should proceed but it doesn't. Why? Because, like change, following the logical path doesn't often work. In this case it was a gradual recognition that the most 'interesting' part of the book would probably be 'Getting there'. So, in order to hook your commitment I have included that section early on! It may not make much logical sense but if it gets you to read on, it is worth it. Like getting energy mobilized for change, we sometimes need to provide a taste of what could be.

Introduction

Why a book on change? Why, particularly, a book entitled *Managing Change and Making It Stick* when it's obvious that change is happening at an ever increasing rate, as we're being constantly told, and also that it's happening in spite of us. This whole situation was summed up wonderfully for me recently when working with a managing director who explained to me that he had spent the last twelve months hoping that things would settle down and get back to normal, and it gradually dawned on him that they already had. Once that realization has taken place we are in a position to begin thinking about how we can *manage* the changes rather than simply survive them and be buffeted by their consequences.

'Managing' is the key word. It means taking control of and shaping the direction, then influencing in some way the outcome, of changes. In some cases, and they are the ones to which this book refers especially, changes have been thought through and initiated by managers in the organizations themselves and in that sense they are – at least partly – planned.

Why is change such a topical subject at the moment? What's happening that makes it more relevant and central to the existence of our organizations than ever before?

We can partly answer these questions by looking around at our society at a number of different levels. If we look at environmental change generally, it is not difficult to see, and feel, the turmoil and movement that exists in what used to be the anchors in our society. We can see it in three distinct but interrelated aspects of our environment – the social, the economic, and the technological.

Paradoxes of unprecedented proportions face us in all these areas. On a world scale in the social sphere we have widespread starvation with northern hemisphere bureaucracy seemingly unable to help and yet massive aid being mobilized by the actions of one rock star. At the national level we have increasing disputes between employed and unemployed, rich and poor, whilst at the same time we continue to fuel the differences by fiscal and legislative actions.

In the economic area we also see unprecedented instability in world currencies, massive defaults and (euphemistically called) rescheduling of major national debts of Third World countries. The IMF no longer seems able to stabilize events and even the major currencies no longer seem to follow the well-established rules. At a UK level we have 'little bangs' and 'big bangs' all heralding upsets and shifts in the traditional boundaries between the financial institutions. Linked to all this is the enormous pace of technological innovation. This is creating major opportunities which were previously inconceivable, but at the same time it is creating massive unemployment and forcing major realignment of job skills and availability of talent.

Add to all this – in the UK at least – a radical government bent on changing basic values about ownership and it is not difficult to see why change comes high on the agenda for discussion. Bringing some semblance of *management* to these change processes can only be helpful in reducing the degree of chaos and felt anxiety which they create.

In the UK the Westland affair and the protracted dispute between the teachers and government illustrate par excellence how not to handle change and influence events successfully. The rights and wrongs of the conflicts themselves are not important to our purpose here. What they both demonstrate powerfully are the dire and expensive consequences of not paying sufficient attention to the ways and means of implementing change. The key factor in both situations has become the *way* in which the people involved *feel* they have been treated. It is how the influencing has been carried out that is driving the pattern of events now, not the principles at stake or the substance of rational argument.

This is mirrored at many levels in our society – in large-scale acquisitions and mergers, company reorganizations, departmental restructuring and so on.

Whenever I become involved in these activities the pattern seems the same. *How* we go about managing – or more often *not* managing – the people involved in, and affected by, the change is always the joker in the pack. The amount of care, time and money expended on that area is directly proportional to the likelihood of success.

This pattern repeats itself not only in organizations but in communities and individual families as well. If I feel manipulated I resent it deeply.

Attempts to influence situations, to create the outcomes wanted, or to change the direction of events by using power, status, manipulation, guile and so on has always been a time-honoured – and in many cases successful – way of doing things. Machiavelli's *The Prince* must be the primer for those seeking practical guidance in this approach! So why is it not working in our developed societies as well as it used to?

One underlying premise of this approach is that those involved in, or affected by, the changes contemplated must be as little involved in the strategy as practically possible. In this way, by the time they realize what is happening it will be a *fait accompli* and they will have relatively few options but to reluctantly accept the new situation. I know of some organizations where employees still expect to be managed in this way and tolerate it in exchange for the comfort of knowing that someone else is taking the important decisions.

But this attitude is rare today. The values, attitudes and responses of individuals and groups of people to this approach are altering. We are no longer prepared to accept being manipulated, influenced, pressured into accepting changes which we don't understand, or which we don't agree with. And what's even more fundamental is that whilst disliking and resenting being manipulated is not a new experience, the willingness to articulate the feeling is increasingly acceptable.

So the difference is not only the sheer volume of change itself but in the attitudes and values of those of us, in the developed world in particular, who are affected. We are becoming increasingly committed to questioning motives, asking for reasons, probing underneath the surface of the smooth logic and rationale provided for the changes. We are seeking the personal satisfaction of knowing that they are making sense for our organizations and are of some benefit to us as individuals as well as to those who are the initiators of the changes.

Later in this book I look at the stages of development of an organization, and reflected in these is the shift in values I am alluding to here. At a national level historically we have lived within an essentially bureaucratic system where a paternalistic state has presented changes for our good. Whilst we may not have wholeheartedly agreed with those changes, the majority of us have tended to take Dr Pangloss's view that 'Everything is for the best in the best of all possible worlds'. This is no longer the case as our values shift towards what I have referred to as the third phase of organization, or the democratic phase. In this stage individuals begin to take responsibility for themselves, to challenge and question, and to think much more independently. The organization is no longer the all-embracing cosy benevolent dictator that it used to be. It is supported only if it deserves it.

There is nothing new in these feelings that people have about the way things are changed. What is new is the extent to which those feelings become strong and articulated and – most important –legitimate.

In consequence, those contemplating bringing about organizational change have to be far more cognizant of the ways and means they use to do so than has ever been the case in the past. It is no longer possible to bring about change by 'slipping one through the system', however cleverly it is done, and hoping that either no one will notice or that they will shrug their shoulders and let it pass. Those involved in the 'government leak' method of influencing events recently will be acutely aware of this point!

This means that the implementation of change, how you actually go about the process of bringing about the conditions for effective change, how you get people's commitment to it and involvement in it, are infinitely more important issues than they were even a decade ago.

Failure to recognize this finds its way straight to the bottom line, and the consequences will last over long periods of time.

The significance of this shift in values and attitudes towards organizations, managers and 'changers' of any sort cannot be over-stressed. The pressure on managers to devote considerably more time and energy not only to the processes of implementing changes but to establishing them and gaining acceptance of them has never been greater – and this even in a high unemployment economy where one might expect more docility.

From the point of view of managers and their organizations, this has very clear implications. It means that those organizations who are prepared to invest time, energy and money in the sensitive and careful managing of change processes are those that will be around longer (other commercial factors being equal) and probably more successfully.

Add to this the dramatically increased pace of change where it is daily more obvious that many organizations don't survive because they are not able to learn and adapt fast enough, and it is clear that we had better get on and do some fast learning about how to manage change in our organizations better.

So the consistent and recurring theme throughout this book is that it is no use whatsoever having a clever, well thought through strategy and tactical plans of *what* you want to change without a parallel strategy and tactical plans for *how* you are going to implement it and make it stick.

This book is entirely about managing the *how*.

SECTION 1

How do we get there?
Planning for implementability of change

Raising the awareness of the need to change, mobilizing the energy to change, working on the development of a vision, engaging in a thorough diagnosis of current reality – these are all statements of intent, not in themselves positive visible actions. They are a means to an end. They are all vital and necessary components of the change process. They help to begin the process of moving and set the climate for implementation. But whilst diagnosis is crucial and necessary it must operate on the principle of parallel implementation. Potential implementers must be involved at every stage in a multitude of ways, otherwise the initial diagnostic stages become the first point of resistance.

Recognize any of these?

'We tried that years ago and it didn't work.'

'Nothing will ever change around here.'

'Things are changing so fast that if we buy one now it will soon be out of date. Let's wait . . .'

'This requires extensive and thorough analysis.'

'A lot of change is just for the sake of change.'

'Organizational change is like pulling up your plants to see how the roots are coming along.'

'If only I had time . . .'

'Plus ça change, plus c'est la même chose.'

'You can't teach old dogs new tricks.'

'We do need to change but the climate is not right just now. Let's wait . . .'

'I have never stood in the way of progress, but . . .'

'There's nothing wrong here that a good upturn in the market wouldn't put right . . .'

17

'With that lot at the top, what's the point!'

'It'll never last.'

Most of us are familiar with, and indeed skilled at, playing the sort of 'resister games' mentioned here. We each have our own favourite versions and as a manager of change I really shouldn't be surprised if I find them used against me.

The two key questions we need to ask are *why* and *how*? Why does resistance exist and where does it come from? How can I work at minimizing or reducing it?

WHY DOES RESISTANCE EXIST?

Without delving deeply into areas of individual psychology, there is a wide range of typical causes of resistance. These are rarely simple cause and effect situations, and resistance is usually a complex mix of historic, factual and emotional issues, which are not always easy to disentangle. However, the following list, while not exhaustive, does mention the most frequent sources of resistance to change and unwillingness to engage in new behaviour.

Fear of the unknown
Lack of information
Misinformation
Historical factors
Threat to core skills and competence
Threat to status
Threat to power base
No perceived benefits
Low trust organizational climate
Poor relationships
Fear of failure
Fear of looking stupid
Reluctance to experiment
Custom bound
Reluctance to let go
Strong peer group norms

Listing the possible causes of resistance can be a useful process in itself since it can be seen that some of them are considerably easier to deal with than others. Low trust may be a key issue but is a considerably longer term proposition to rectify than correcting misinformation or reassuring staff about training in new skills.

Resistance comes essentially in two forms – systemic and behavioural. Systemic resistance arises from lack of appropriate knowledge, information, skills and managerial capacity. Behavioural resistance describes resistance deriving from the reactions, perceptions and assumptions of individuals or groups in the organization. So one is cognitive and the other emotional, a distinction I find useful because it allows me to see that some resistance sources are easier to correct and minimize than others. As already noted, an emotionally based resistance such as low trust is much more difficult to handle than a lack of information or misunderstanding of facts.

Levels of resistance will inevitably be higher if the levels of involvement and information are low. This is the essence of parallel implementation. The less I know about plans to change, the more I assume, the more suspicious I become, and the more I direct my energy into the counterproductive 'resister games' referred to above. Once I feel manipulated, or uninvolved, I will inevitably tend to veer towards a negative view of the change and its effect on me.

The management of resistance demands attention to the systemic aspects such as information and communication flow, which need to be considerably increased during the uncertainty of the change process. It also demands attention to the natural individual and group processes of prejudice, assumption perception and conclusion formation, because these processes will take place with or without 'facts'.

You need to pay attention to those weak signals which indicate bigger problems to come. It is at this early stage in the change process that as a change manager you have a golden opportunity to turn feelings of threat – and hence resistance – into perceptions of opportunity and benefit.

In my experience, one of the most common resistance patterns, which is not always easy to recognize until it is too late, is the 'paralysis by analysis' syndrome, especially in organizations which consist of highly intelligent, rational people with a great leaning towards the intellectual enjoyment of the analysis process for its own sake. There is nothing quite as satisfying as doing a good diagnosis which is rigorous and wide-reaching. The problem is always that it gets out of phase with changing realities, so that the longer the diagnostic phase takes, the greater the chances are of the goal posts having been moved. There is ample evidence of this having happened – sometimes by default or lack of awareness but, in my own experience, sometimes by deliberate tactic of those who want to get on with the changes whilst others are kept busy diagnosing. Blackler & Brown make reference in their evaluative study of Shell UK's company philosophy to the relative 'failure' of the organization's Refining Board to take on board the new style of management and point to an overlong diagnostic phase as one of the key factors in this 'failure'. They also make the valid point that long diagnostic periods tend also to raise expectations unrealistically about outcomes.

The significant point here for the change manager is that he can inadvertently be seduced into reinforcing this process out of sheer intellectual curiosity and unwittingly find himself colluding in avoiding action. The seductiveness of the analysis game is that there is a very thin line between a good thorough analysis and avoiding action. There is always a good reason for getting more data and thus putting off implementation. Never forget what you are doing it *for*. Making it happen is what is important.

HOW TO MAKE CHANGE HAPPEN

A very simple but powerful technique is time budgeting. Simply cost out roughly the amount of time, based on salaries, spent on each phase of the change process. Time in meetings, interviewing, designing questionnaires, etc. Just as you would when paying your consultancy bills. It can sharpen the mind wonderfully.

I recently spent time with the directors of a large savings bank in Sweden. They have been undergoing a series of major changes which have involved both structure and culture change on a significant scale. They appear to have managed the process with considerable care and sensitivity. They did, however, describe one event which highlights admirably the diagnostic dilemma. Shortly after the beginning of the process in early 1983, an action group was set up consisting of some senior managers and a consultant. Potentially a very powerful group, it was charged with the task of reporting to top management on change strategy and tactics. The group buried itself in its task with verve and commitment, clearly forgot to pay attention to the management of its boundary with the rest of the organization and by the time it laid its well matured 'egg' in January 1984, it caused considerable disruption in the flow of the change process. The world had moved on. By the end of 1983 a management plan had already evolved in the usual pragmatic, piecemeal way and had begun to be implemented.

This is a good example of what can happen when the *task* of diagnosis becomes so seductive that the *process* of managing the interface with the rest of the world gets forgotten. It is a problem which, over the years, many service departments have experienced with their user departments for much the same reasons. Managing concrete technical tasks is so much easier than managing behaviour and behavioural processes.

This example is especially relevant since in every other way the changes in this organization seem to have been managed remarkably well, right from total staff involvement by the managing director at the start of the process. But even in a climate where the human processes are consciously managed, tasks still have a nasty habit of seducing their masters.

> UNLESS BEHAVIOUR CHANGES
> NOTHING CHANGES

It is patently nonsensical to suggest that change processes are so clearcut and predictable that the beginning of the 'making it happen' phase can be clearly identified. For ease of discussion, however, I shall refer to it as if this were the case. As long as we do not fool ourselves into believing the world is really like that, the concept will remain useful to us.

So what are the main questions that need to be answered in the 'making it happen' phase of a change process?

— Influencing behaviour – what are the leverage points in the organization?
— Blockages and resistances – what are they and how can they be managed?
— What power do I have – how can I best use it?
— How can I learn from the process?
— How 'ready' for change is the system?
— What about strategies and tactics?

HOW TO REDUCE RESISTANCE

Influencing behaviour

Don't underestimate your ability or potential to influence. It is no accident that the law on conspiracy, which has been around a very long time, recognizes the power of a very few people to influence events. It states that illegal conspiracy requires 'the agreement of *two or more persons* to do an unlawful act or to do a lawful act by unlawful means'. It has long been known that two people together can be a very powerful force for change. In the next chapter we look at feelings of powerlessness. In terms of overcoming that by building networks and alliances, this powerful legal reminder should not be underestimated.

In this section we look in detail at your role and style as an influencer, the way in which your influence will vary depending on your style and experience.

The influencing *process* is our major concern here since, if we are to change anything, it involves persuading people to behave differently to the way they have done in the past. How can they be influenced to do this? We know *what* has to change, at least in broad terms; what we need to do now is decide *how*. This brings us right back to parallel implementation again. One of the most important motive forces in altering behaviour is the *process of involvement* in the organizational change and the development of the reasons for it. At the other end of the spectrum there is the ancient human motive of *survival*. If there is a choice, and there may not always be, the involvement strategy is much more likely to result in long-term behaviour change.

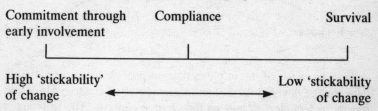

Range of motives for changing behaviour

Commitment through early involvement	Compliance	Survival

High 'stickability' of change   Low 'stickability' of change

Likelihood of long-term
behaviour change

The behaviour change process starts at, or before, the 'conception' stage, not at 'birth'. Two issues to be addressed here are *who* needs to be influenced and *how*.

Who should be influenced?

A method I have found extremely useful in this regard is a process I call Key Relationship Mapping. This involves considering issues concerned solely with the successful implementation of a change project (the 'making change happen' that was referred to earlier). It requires a number of key questions to be asked about these individuals, or groups of people, who will need to be influenced and supportive if the change is to go ahead and remain in place over the longer term.

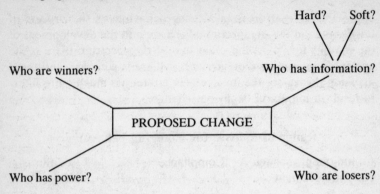

Hard?   Soft?

Who are winners?   Who has information?

PROPOSED CHANGE

Who has power?   Who are losers?

   This diagnosis of the implementation process provides valuable data for the development of an implementation strategy alongside the more technical details of the change content. The four areas mentioned above are starting points which lead into other areas of useful thought.

Winners and Losers

These are individuals, or perhaps departments, who will clearly benefit in some way from a change or who *perceive* themselves as winners, or the reverse. This area provides wide scope for developing appropriate informational or educational strategies aimed at changing perceptions. Those groups who see themselves as losers may be persuaded that there are certain benefits to be gained from supporting the change. It is an area likely to be much more characterized by the subtlety of beliefs and assumptions than by facts. So the provision of information and support in this area to the right people could be worth considerable effort, especially during the periods of high uncertainty prior to change taking place. Finding opinion shapers is an important activity at this stage as they will need to be the prime focus of management energy.

   I became involved some years ago in a change project where a decision-making process through various departments in an organization took, typically, six to nine months. Each of the seven departments involved worked on their own aspect of the data, passed it up to their manager who in turn passed it on to the next manager in the sequence, who then gave it to his people to work on, and so on. What we did was very simple. We created a small project team drawn from each of the departments concerned and put them together to work on the task. Result? Excellent quality decision in nine weeks. But we had paid very little attention to the needs of the departmental heads, apart from keeping them informed and assuming that they would be delighted to bathe in the reflected glory of this 'success' story. Wrong. They saw themselves as losers because they had lost their control and their power base. The project worked only once, then reverted back to the previous system for all sorts of 'sound, rational' reasons. The system of project teams is now accepted and working in that company but not while most of those managers were still in post.

Our failure was to underestimate the needs of the losers and to have no strategy for turning them into winners wherever possible. In this case it was especially important because the 'losers' had considerable power to veto the change.

Who has information?

This aspect can be the real sticking point of any change. In order to carry out the detailed planning of the change process, information about what exists now and where we want to be is necessary. First of all *hard information* is required about volumes, prices, structures, stocks, manpower levels or whatever. Equally important is to establish who are the gatekeepers of the *soft information* such as 'How does one go about approaching Mr X about sensitive issues in his department?' or 'How reliable or competent is Joe Bloggs?' or 'Who knows how this section *really* works?' Access to both these types of information is going to be crucial before you even begin planning a change process. The act of asking is the first step in implementation.

Who Has the Power?

This really concerns the hidden part of the iceberg that we shall be referring to in more detail later, in the sense that it does not always follow that the chief executive is the person with the power. In a hi- tech company it may be the brilliant boffin who has all the data, or the person who is closest to major customers in a retail oriented company. As an interesting aside the most powerful groups in many retail operations have, historically, been the buying departments, which has caused some problems, with this sector putting up powerful resistance to change.

In the last analysis, as the agent or manager of change, I need to know who can abort the process or, conversely, whose patronage I need – if only passively – to carry it through. I recently visited a large company in the West Bengal province of India. In this part of India trade unions are very powerful, active and extreme. The power in the organization was heavily embedded in the personnel managers, because they controlled that key interface on which all else depended. Whether this is right or wrong is not the issue. Recognizing where the power lies is paramount. Making any changes in that organization will require the support of the personnel function. Going to the top in this case will not be enough.

Networking and managing coalitions

Once this process of Key Relationship Mapping has been done it provides ample data on which to base an action plan for beginning to build your influence networks. It tells you where you need to massage connections with particular individuals or groups, which meetings you should attend as priority and where to direct your limited time and energy resources.

It also enables you to see whether there are any unholy alliances or coalitions you need to nurture. Perhaps those people in key power roles who have the information need to be somehow brought together with potential winners in order to surround the 'losers'. Maybe powerful groups of implementers down in the organization need to be brought into contact with senior initiators of change in some way, so that parallel implementation can begin to take place.

There may be power bases outside your immediate organization, but with strong influence on decision-makers, that you could call into play, such as unions, professional bodies, political groups and so on.

All these options will be clearer once the mapping process has been thought through.

A case of poor map reading

In a large multinational company based in South East Asia a new MD arrived. His brief was to move the organization of 5,000 people 'into the twentieth century'. The structure of the company was traditional and hierarchical, with many of the senior functional managers having been in posts for up to ten years or more. These were the managers immediately below board level. One symbol of the company's colonial style of operation and culture was the company car scheme. All senior managers were provided with company cars and some junior managers and operational staff also had them. The situation was not uncommon. Senior managers drove their company cars, on average, 1–2 miles to and from the office every day, whilst many operational staff often had to wait hours to get a pool car to drive to an outlying site for inspection of equipment.

This was a potentially highly emotive issue – as are all company car schemes. The MD decided to change this system to one based, largely, on operational need rather than status. His first step was to seek relevant information from his senior functional managers so that a decision could be made as to degrees of operational usage of cars, mileage, cost, depreciation information and so on. He allowed several weeks for the information to be collected and announced that the decisions would be based on the data provided by the various departments. Several weeks passed and no information was forthcoming. After several more weeks of delay and 'extraordinary' business pressure on other matters on the part of the senior managers, the MD began to get the message that they were not going to play the game. The 'soggy sponge' was at work!

Had the MD carried out even a simple Key Relationship Mapping exercise on the back of an envelope he could have predicted the outcome and tuned his strategy accordingly. All the cards were stacked against him.

As a new MD entering a well-established system, he had little power. The power lay at senior functional levels. The MD had little or no access to information, hard or soft, and, even more crucial, those managers who had the power saw themselves clearly as losers.

In this situation, where the power source is the loser, it is wise to think again. Either determine to make smaller changes over a longer period or, even better, look for something else to change – unless you are able, or prepared, simply to use 'muscle'. If you do, get ready for the backlash either in the short or the long term!

The 'soggy sponge' phenomenon

This is a phenomenon which occurs time and time again. It has to do predominantly with where the power and information lies in the organization. Almost every change strategy that has ever been developed has, in some way or other, to contend with the 'soggy sponge'.

It is the layer of management usually below the top, but at quite senior functional level. It usually consists of very competent, well-established managers who run the organization, and often have done so for many years. They, between them, operate the flow valves which regulate information and communication up and down and across the organization. As the MD in the above ex- ample found out to his cost, little can be achieved on your own. Why soggy sponge? Because this group has the unique capacity to absorb information as it flows to and fro. While it can shield the board from information as it travels up, it can also filter it down as it chooses. This makes the group exceedingly powerful. The analogy does not stop there because sponges when they are full of water become very 'soggy', heavy and immobile. A layer of man- agement at this level, which is allowed to control information and behave in this way will eventually stifle the organization's creative energy and may need to be cleared away or 'squeezed dry'.

In terms of focus of influence during changes, whilst the com- mon exhortation is to start with commitment from the top this, in my experience, is not enough. At least a fair proportion of support from the 'soggy sponge' is absolutely necessary. This may well involve either lengthening the timescale of the change or, if that is not possible, a commitment to remove all or some of that layer of management. Unless removing or 'squeezing' the soggy sponge is the target of the change, then the strategy might, of course, need to be somewhat different.

Managing blockages and resistances

We shall be looking later at the organization as an open system and we shall see that attempts to induce changes in such a system are likely to result in some form of blocking or resisting so as to maintain the status quo. The important fact to remember is that *resistance to change is a natural phenomenon*. It does not come from sheer cussedness, it needs to be recognized, understood and managed. This is true of organizational and departmental systems as well as of individuals.

Sources of resistance are worthy of some further examination since it is such a common fact of life which managers either experience themselves or have to deal with in others. The main problem with resistance is that it is not a rational process and, therefore, cannot often be managed by using logic. It is emotionally rooted and the sources of the resistance need to be explored. Lewin's widely used Force Field Analysis framework is one very useful way of diagnosing this area. It also, more importantly, provides us with insight into what steps need to be taken to begin to deal with resistance. And it is a very useful process to work through with a group as a parallel implementation process. Doing it overtly serves to build trust and reduce resistance.

Let us consider a typical organizational problem – the need to increase quality of service, whether it be to another department or the customer outside the organization. Force field theory tells us that the situation (i.e. current level of service, in this case) is kept in 'quasi-equilibrium' by a field of forces – some driving towards change and some resisting change.

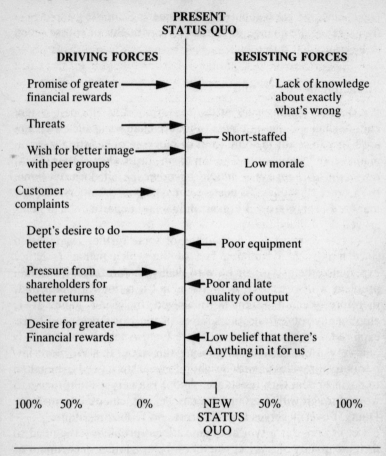

The example given above is the sort of force field map that can typically be drawn. In reality many more specific factors can be identified and can also be weighted in terms of their relative importance or strength. The strength of force is indicated by length of the line drawn.

If we ask the question, 'What typically happens in an organization when there is a problem?' the answer will, more often than

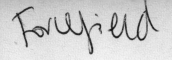

not, be 'fix it' not 'understand it'. This is where the force field concept is so helpful because it provides two distinct courses of action rather than one. There is the 'action' manager's natural tendency to 'drive it through' or 'push it along', but force field helps us realize that the more we push or drive, the more we increase the resisting forces on the other side of the equation.

So now we have a choice. We can move around to the other side of the equation and expend some energy finding out more about the resisting forces. What are they? Where do they come from? Why are they there? The very process of *listening actively* to the resisting forces will have the effect of reducing them. *Then* the driving forces can be given a nudge and movement will begin.

Let's see what might be done with the map above.

Building an action strategy

On the driving force side there are a number of forces which could be regarded as positive and some negative. Begin by considering the strongest driving forces which could be construed as positive: customer complaints; desire for better financial rewards; dept's desire to do better.

Here we already have the basis for some interesting options. How can customer complaints be presented to the group in question in a way which will encourage self-analysis and thought rather than defensiveness? Linked to the need for better and more timely feedback on performance output we already have the basis of a useful strategy. Link this to some concrete statements about how incremental improvements will lead not only to more positive rewards but also better image with peer groups, and you have begun to make progress. Now we can concentrate on the strongest resisting forces and begin to set up mechanisms for reducing those. Meetings, discussions, information, targets, possible support in key staff areas, training, etc. Soon a new equilibrium will be found by focusing on a combination of driving and resisting forces, and by using resistance not as a threat but as an opportunity. Those of you who engage in Judo or other martial art forms will understand this process very well because the use of balancing forces is the very basis of such activity. Resistance is not 'overcome', it is 'managed'.

The key is avoiding the temptation to rush into offensive action and to spend some time *listening and understanding*. It will save a lot of energy being wasted and ulcers being aggravated. My favourite quote is from the president of a French medical company when he explained to me: *'Our problem, in essence, is a simple one. We never have time to do anything, but we always seem to find time to do it twice!'*

To summarize, the six activities which are central to effective change implementation, and which will be explained and expanded upon in the future sections of the book, are as follows.

THE SIX KEY ACTIVITIES FOR SUCCESSFUL IMPLEMENTATION

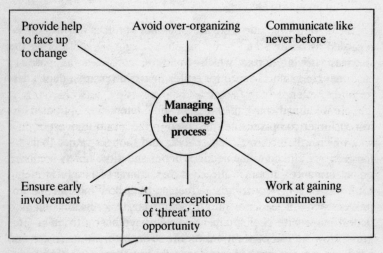

Provide help to face up to change

Avoid over-organizing

Communicate like never before

Managing the change process

Ensure early involvement

Turn perceptions of 'threat' into opportunity

Work at gaining commitment

1. Helping individuals or groups face up to change

This involves taking them through the crisis stages towards reality acceptance of the need to change. (This approach is discussed more fully in the section 'Where are we now?'). It also requires the organization to reward and encourage risk-taking to the extent that learning begins to take place. Scapegoats are not sought, but lessons for the future are learned. A culture which has encouraged flexibility and movement of people is more likely to succeed in helping to face change than one where functional rigidity has been the order of the day.

If, as often happens, certain individuals are likely to be confirmed opponents to change come what may, then their direct role in the change process should be minimized. Surround them rather than make a full frontal assault with your heavy artillery. They will either retire gracefully from the field or eventually join the winning side. Equally, time needs to be given to supporting and reinforcing those who are positive to ensure their maximum co- operation and initiative.

A common strategy I use for managing resistant senior managers is to accede to their desire not to become involved in early developmental activities or projects but to ensure that they are kept fully informed of progress. There inevitably comes a point where they feel increasingly isolated from colleagues and find face-saving ways of joining the party – especially if it's going well.

2. Communicate like you have never communicated before

Extra special effort needs to be made to pump communications especially hard during change efforts. Anything that reduces uncertainty to an acceptable level will help. Likewise, too much secrecy and complacency will hinder progress. This is often neglected, or feared, in case panic is created or pre-emptive strikes by the opposition are mobilized. The risk of leaving a vacuum is much greater. All that happens is that the grapevine fills the vacuum with wild rumour and misinformation. Downward information is important but pumping feedback up the organization is even more crucial to effective implementation. There is more information down in the organization relevant to effectively implementing changes than you have at your level, so use it. Information flow between departments is also crucial and the whole package of formal and informal communication at your disposal should be mobilized (see the case of International Chemicals on p. 66).

3. Gaining energetic commitment to the change

In the long term, this can only come from the system reward structures, employment policies and management practices, which operate in the organization. In the short term, however, it can be encouraged by focusing sharply on the importance of the change to the survival and success of the organization, which often requires some sort of 'common vision' to be created of what could be, and by the time-honoured tactic of focusing on the external 'enemy'. The competition often provides this thrust.

4. Early involvement

As has been mentioned many times during this book, early involvement in the formulation of the change will go a long way towards reducing behavioural resistance during implementation. It will reduce considerably the amount of energy which has to be expended on coercion and power strategies to enforce compliance.

5. Opportunity or threat? A perception of change

There is consistent evidence that organizations which encourage the perception of change as a natural, continuing and 'opportunity providing' aspect of their existence are much more likely to benefit from change and manage resistance effectively.

6. Avoid over-organizing

This can occur in organizations which recognize the reality that they cannot totally control the change process. The Swedish bank mentioned previously learned this the hard way. At the start of their major change process they mapped out in great structural detail what the future bank organization would look like. In the event, this detail severely clogged up the change process and they felt, in retrospect, that one major lesson they learned was the need to have a clear but relatively generalized vision and to allow the detailed structure, procedures and systems to evolve during the process of changing. It is not easy to surrender the traditional managerial activity of planning down to the last detail, but if it is done, it gives management the flexibility to adapt quickly, as necessary.

An analogy is sailing a boat from point A to point B. It is vital to keep clearly in mind the objective – to get to point B. However, the chances of getting there directly are remote, given the vagaries of wind, current and tide. What has to be done is to have the flexibility to tack with the wind but at the same time not to lose sight of the ultimate objective – point B.

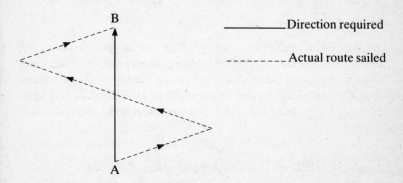

The long tacks en route may either be regarded as irritating diversions from the main purpose, or as opportunities to consolidate, influence or build support ready for the eventual success of the change mission.

The trick is to keep your eye firmly on the objective and to have the necessary skill to pick up signals and 'hooks' which enable you to keep a 'fix' on the next tack without losing a sense of direction. This is another situation in which key information from down in the organization, just as much as from the environment outside, is essential so that the navigation can be as accurate as possible.

These six key areas of activity are clearly not the whole story. They are, however, crucial aspects of successful implementation strategies and will therefore crop up continuously throughout this book in various forms. They all depend on one common factor – the skill and sensitivity you will demonstrate in *how* you carry out the activities. This means that it all depends on your behaviour, your skills, your awareness of yourself and others, and the situation you are in. Since you will likely be the prime mover in some change situations, we shall start next by focusing on three aspects of your own behaviour, which are especially relevant to change management – learning, power and influence.

SECTION 2

Change starts with you

Whilst a great deal of this book focuses on organizational change, it is not possible to do so in the abstract. The basic unit of change must be the individual, and how better or more appropriate than to focus our attention on you, the individual manager, as our starting point.

So let us begin by exploring some of the issues you face in an organization if you want to influence in some way the course of events to bring about change. These issues will be partly to do with the nature of the organization, and partly to do with the way you interact with it.

How well-equipped are you? We know quite a lot about the ideal characteristics required for a manager to survive and succeed in a changing environment. Characteristics such as openness to new information, flexibility, the capacity to rise above the surface and survey the whole scene – known as 'helicopter' quality (not to mention balloon quality, the ability to rise to the top on hot air!), the ability to collect and analyse valid data.

The vital question, however, is not whether we can sit in an armchair and recognize the characteristics but whether we are able to *do it*. This depends on our ability to *learn*, to use *power*, and to *influence* effectively from our role.

LEARNING AND CHANGE

Simply put, it's what we *do* that counts, not what we know or talk about. So how can we get a handle on our propensity to behave in a certain way in a change situation? The factor most likely to influence our capacity to change is our capacity to learn. The learning process is a key to managing change both in ourselves and in our organizations, and is worthy of further exploration. One stage of the learning process is no more important than another, all are equally interdependent. The four stages of learning are:

37

1. Data collection
2. Reflection and analysis
3. Vision and concept-building
4. Action

Let's look briefly at each stage in turn.

Data collection

Clearly, without good data we don't get very far. As a manager, especially in a change situation with its fast pace and many uncertainties, the pressure is on. This often means you will be tempted to short-cut the data collection process by relying too heavily on your own experience. It is a valid source of data, but it is only one source. The manager who is skilful at data collection will use as many sources as he can – bosses, subordinates, colleagues, clients, customers, suppliers, statistical sources, and so on. Don't forget that data comes in two very different types. Hard factual data and what I call soft data, such as impressions, gut feelings, morale, cultural dimensions of the organization. So the quality and quantity of data available is vast, and being good at tapping into it means using all your senses. You need to develop *big ears for weak signals*. These are the rumblings, whether from the environment or elsewhere in your own system, which signal that a major upheaval could well take place if action is not taken to smooth or defuse it. The 'small-eared' manager will not deal with it until the rumble gets louder – if he hears it at all. By then he will be doing his impression of the captain of the *Titanic*. 'We were given two eyes, two ears and one mouth. *Used in those proportions* they are the change manager's best tools.'

Things you can do to improve the quality of your personal database

— Go and *listen* to new recruits, *not talk* to them.
— Phone the office when you are away somewhere – switchboard efficiency is revealing.
— Join new people for lunch or sport.

— Talk to chauffeurs, porters, tea ladies.
— Treat management secretaries as part of management.
— Listen to the grapevine, it's rarely wrong (completely!).
— Walk around.
— Smile more often – they'll tell you much more.

Reflection and analysis

Collecting the data is fine but you now have to do something with it. Time must be made to think about it, to sift, sort and analyze it. The increasing trend in organizations for senior teams to go off site for short periods of time is a recognition of the need to take time out to reflect and analyze without pressure of day-to-day crises interfering. Often the only time a manager gets to reflect is going home in the car or on the train – or perhaps in the bath.

Vision and concept-building

Having collected and sifted the data so that it begins to make some sort of sense, the next stage is to apply an overall framework to it. This often can take the form of longer-term goals, mission statements, visions and, indeed, theories about how to achieve them. It is at this stage that strategies are formulated.

Action

This is the stage where implementation takes place. Others actually see the physical manifestation of whatever reflection or vision-building has gone before, if indeed there has been any!

These are the four stages in the learning sequence. It surely sounds very logical and obvious. My experience shows that life isn't like that. I, for example, score very strongly on data collection, reflection and action but have a low score on plans and concepts. What does this mean in practice? It means that I will be a good listener, I will think, reflect, observe – then be strongly driven to go out and try it, to experiment. I will tend to miss out the stage of concept-building, planning and strategy development. The important point is that once I am aware of that potential weak spot I can compensate for it, to some degree.

For many managers the pattern is a different one. Strong on data collection, especially their own past experience, weak on reflection, concept development and planning, strong on action. The pressure to manage day-to-day activities and to be seen to take action, together with the natural preferences mentioned, means that reflection and concept-building are often lowly valued activities in many organizations. So, what happens in practice is that as soon as one of these 'Action Man' managers gets some data he short circuits and is triggered straight into a response. The 'Action Man' trap. This is, in my experience, the most common behaviour pattern in managerial circles. Learning then becomes a process of trial and error. The reflective manager has different problems. He spends so much time collecting, checking, sifting data that by the time action is contemplated the world has moved on. Our friends in the Swedish bank working party seem to have been caught in this trap – maybe they hadn't got an 'Action Man' in the team.

It is helpful to be realistic about one's own preferences on this model. No one is perfect and we each have a bias in a particular direction which will lead us towards over-emphasis on one or more of these factors. Being aware of these biases can help us to compensate for them and operate in a more balanced way.

This is important data because if managers, as a basic unit of change in the organization, are not effective learners, the organization itself will not learn and *organizations that don't learn at a faster rate than their environment changes will eventually die*.

WHAT POWER DO YOU HAVE AND HOW DO YOU USE IT?

One of the recurring themes in this book will be power and influence. An understanding of power and how it can be used to influence changes is vital to you in bringing about changes successfully. While we are focusing on you as the agent of change it would be well to look at the power you have and how you use it.

In change situations there is always a need to influence key actors once targets for change have been identified. Over the last decade or so there has been an increasing interest in the concept of power in management theory but this has been accompanied by a noticeable 'creep' of feelings of powerlessness further up the organization hierarchy. Back in the late 1960s and early 1970s I was already finding considerable evidence of middle and junior managers feeling powerless to influence larger organizations. These feelings of powerlessness seem to be seeping further and further up the organization and appear with increasing regularity at very senior functional levels. This has serious consequences for an organization seeking to change but it need not be so. There is power to be had, provided one knows where to find it and how to harness it. First of all, though, let's look at where these feelings of powerlessness come from, how they can be overcome and what their consequences are for changing organizations.

Phrases like 'What can I do?' or 'It's my boss you should be convincing' seem to crop up endlessly. So why does this happen? It is certainly not a new phenomenon. Eric Fromm in *Fear of Freedom* (1942) outlined the situation very starkly in relation to taking responsibility for oneself and one's own actions.

'To feel completely alone and isolated leads to mental disintegration just as physical starvation leads to death. This relatedness to others is not identical with physical contact. An individual may be alone in the physical sense for many years and yet he may be related to ideals, values, or at least a social system that gives him a feeling of communion and "belongingness". On the other hand he may live among people and yet be overcome with an utter feeling of isolation.'

At the individual level, the most powerful weapon we have is *choice*, but as Fromm eloquently points out, exercising that choice can, sometimes, be a frightening experience and requires a few good friends and a lot of support – especially when that choice flies in the face of established norms and managerial practice in the organization.

I spend some of my time working with managers on the issue of whether they have any choices in their jobs. Sometimes it's difficult to see, sometimes they don't *want* to see it. For example, a senior manager in an engineering company complained about the quality of performance of his staff. When we discussed it further it transpired that he had over the last three years accepted (out of a management team of ten) four managers on lateral transfer from other parts of the company into key jobs in his team. He knew they were not good performers and that they had been 'dumped' on him by relieved colleagues.

Why had he not refused to accept them? For him the choice was inconceivable. One just didn't do it. He foresaw loss of friendship with colleagues and the risk of being seen as a trouble-maker by his board member. Gradually and painfully he was helped to realize that he was actually seen by his colleagues as a 'soft touch', and by his boss as allowing his department's performance to slip.

This led us to explore the next, quite painful option which he really would rather have avoided: that he could choose to set about improving the performance of the four managers concerned, who incidentally were happily ignorant of how badly their performance was being rated.

This is perhaps an extreme example but I find situations like it very common; personal power of choice is constantly under-estimated.

Seeman in 1971 pointed out that 'experienced powerlessness generates alienation and depression'. He then went on to define six different ways of experiencing such powerlessness:

1. *Individual powerlessness*   I have no control over my own life. It is not within my power to decide my own future. Destiny is in the hands of external forces such as luck, or fate, or the government.

2. *Meaninglessness* My life is absurd, incomprehensible. Nothing I do seems to make any sense. Even if I like to change society, I don't understand how or why things happen. Somebody must have an answer somewhere.

3. *Normlessness (cynicism)*   Normal methods don't produce results. If you want to get anywhere in this life you are going to have to cut a few corners. Hard work never made anybody rich or famous.

4. *Cultural estrangement*   There must be something more to life than money. Whoever set up the priorities in our society ought to have his head examined, or his books audited. I pity the kid who has to grow up in this country.

5. *Self-estrangement*   I haven't lived up to my own expectations. I am not at all what I would like to be or ought to be. I am not really involved in anything I do.

6. *Social isolation*   I feel so lonely, excluded. I'd like to call some friend but I'm not sure I have any. I don't really feel accepted as a person.

These six descriptions of behaviours and attitudes relating to feelings of powerlessness are very potent. They provide insight into some of the possible causes, at the individual level, of impotence and lack of responsibility for self amongst managers. I am sure many of us are able, in varying degrees, to identify with at least some of these statements. Not surprisingly, in a way, since most managers become managers not long before, or during, the onset of middle age when these feelings are more likely to be prevalent. I find that 'self-estrangement' and 'individual powerlessness' are most frequently expressed, and these are certainly blocks to taking power into one's own hands and acting.

If these are bases for feelings of powerlessness, from where can you draw power? There are five main sources of power for the individual manager.

It can clearly be seen that some of these sources of power will have more relevance to your situation than others. For example, if you run your own business in a market where jobs are difficult to get for your employees you might get away with using coercive power. However, it is a short-term proposition and will not ensure long- term commitment. A combination of the others is most likely to be successful in implementing change. Connection power in particular is the one most under-utilized. This is the source of power most widely available to all of us through the careful cultivation of networks of relationships and there is increasing evidence that successful managers are good at this aspect of their power repertoire, whereas less successful managers tend to ignore

---

Five sources of a manager's power

COERCIVE POWER Power to create fear by use of threats or punishment.

EXPERT POWER Power from special knowledge which others need and do not possess. Respect for, and need for, this knowledge creates compliance.

ROLE POWER Power through the position you hold and the associated authority.

REWARD POWER Power to reward financially and to promote or recognize.

CONNECTION POWER Power from social access and network membership upwards, downwards and sideways in the organization.

---

it. In my experience, effective managers, especially at the top of organizations, spend an inordinate amount of time networking, talking informally, building links and relationships. Having done this they then begin to build their strategic agenda – the two or three central things they want to change – and the carefully cultivated network becomes the prime vehicle for implementation over time.

Energy expended on building connections is repaid many times over in commitment and support during implementation.

Role power is the other area where there is good scope for developing a stronger power base since many of us don't exploit the power inherent in our positions as much as we might.

THE POWER OF ROLE

The role you are allocated or carve out for yourself in the organization has a considerable impact on your ability to influence your surroundings and to be an effective change agent. There are a number of aspects of an individual's role which together determine how effective that role is and, in turn, whether it provides a good power base from which the incumbent can influence.

Most managers do not fill their role. By that I mean they do not exercise the power, or use the connections, that their role legitimately allows them in carrying out their job. Most of us operate in a small central area of the role which we can call a 'zone of comfort'. Within this zone of comfort we feel quite safe because we are very sure of our ground and it is a low-risk area. Once we step outside this comfort zone the ground is considerably less firm underfoot. These swampy areas are at the boundary of our expertise, professional knowledge, authority and confidence. The more a manager can expand his zone of comfort, the greater the circle of potential power he has.

Aspects of role

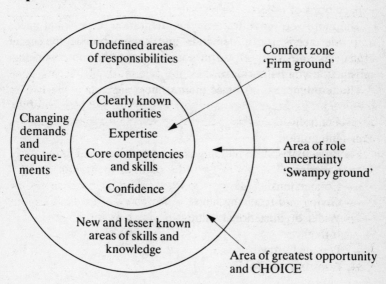

THE TEN DIMENSIONS OF ROLE EFFECTIVENESS

This is a very useful and practical framework which I use regularly with managers (based on an original concept by Udai Pareek) for assessing how effectively they fulfil their roles. There are ten key areas for examination. They focus on two interacting factors that significantly affect the quality of your performance as a manager in your organization: *your potential effectiveness* and *the role you perform*. It is the integration of your potential effectiveness and your role that ensures effective role performance.

You need job knowledge, skills and technical competence in varying combinations to perform effectively (they are assumed here) but they alone are not enough. If your role does not allow you to use your competencies or if you feel constantly frustrated in your role, your performance effectiveness will be low.

Finding out more about the ten factors influencing role effectiveness will enable you to take more initiatives in shaping your role creatively to integrate better your own needs and the expectations of others.

The more you move towards the integration of personal needs and role needs (both demands and expectations), the more effectively you will perform in your role and the more personal satisfaction you will achieve.

The ten dimensions of role effectiveness are:

— Centrality
— Integration
— Proactivity
— Creativity
— Connections
— Giving and receiving help
— Wider organizational value
— Influence
— Personal growth
— Confronting problems

1. Centrality

If persons occupying a particular role in the organization generally feel that the role they occupy is central to the organization, role effectiveness is likely to be high. If persons occupying a particular role feel that their role is peripheral to the mainstream of the organization their potential effectiveness will be low. This is true not only of persons at a high level in the organization but also of people at the lowest levels.

2. Integration

Every person has a particular strength – experience, technical training, special skills, some unique contribution. The more the role a person occupies provides an opportunity for the use of such special strengths, the higher the role effectiveness is likely to be. This is called self-role integration. The self and the role become integrated through the person's use of special strengths in the role. In one organization, a person was promoted to a responsible position that was seen as a coveted prize and was at first quite happy. However, he soon discovered that in the new position he occupied he was not able to use his training, counselling and diagnostic skills. In spite of the fact that he worked very well in the new role, his effectiveness was not as high as it had been in the previous job. When the role was redesigned to enable him to use his skills, his effectiveness went up. Because all of us want our special strengths to be used so that we can demonstrate how effective we can be, integration contributes to high role effectiveness. The most role-effective fathers allow themselves to play trains from time to time!

3. Proactivity

A person will respond to various expectations that people in the organization have of his or her role. This gives the individual a certain satisfaction, and it also satisfies others in the organization. However, if a person is able to take some initiative in his or her role, effectiveness will be higher. Reactive behaviour (responding to the expectations of others) helps a person to be effective to some extent, but proactivity (taking initiatives) generates much more effectiveness. If a person would like to take initiatives but has no opportunity to do so in the role, his or her effectiveness will be low.

4. Creativity

An opportunity to try new and unconventional ways of solving problems or to be creative is just as important as initiative. In an international oil company, junior engineers in the development of potential drilling sites were encouraged to look for ways of speeding up the time from initial survey to exploration drilling and this was reduced from eight months to eight weeks! Not only did the satisfaction of these people go up, but some innovative systems emerged. The opportunity that people were given to be creative and to try innovative ideas increased their role effectiveness and their performance.

5. Connections

If one's role is connected to other roles in the organization, effectiveness will be increased. If there is a joint effort to understand problems and find solutions, the effectiveness of the various roles involved is likely to be high. Similarly, if a person is a member of a task group set up for a specific purpose, his effectiveness, other factors being the same, is likely to be high. The feeling of isolation if a person works without any connection to other roles reduces role effectiveness.

6. Giving and receiving help

In addition to connections, the opportunity for people to receive and give help also increases role effectiveness. If people performing a particular role feel that they can get help from some source in the organization whenever they have such a need, they are likely to have higher role effectiveness. On the other hand, if no help is given when asked for, or if respondents are hostile, role effectiveness will be low. A helping relationship requires both the expectation that help will be available when it is needed and the willingness to respond to the needs of others.

7. Wider organizational value

When a person performing a particular role feels that the role he or she carries out is likely to be of value to a larger group, that person's effectiveness is likely to be high. The roles that give people opportunities to work for 'superordinate' goals have the highest role effectiveness. 'Superordinate' goals serve large groups and cannot be achieved without some collaborative effort.

Some people have voluntarily accepted reduced salaries to move from the top level of the private sector to the public sector mainly because the new role gave them an opportunity to serve a larger interest. Thus, roles in which people feel that what they are doing is helpful to the organization in general usually provide for a fairly high degree of role effectiveness.

8. Influence

The influence a person is able to exercise in his or her organizational role is related to the wider organizational value mentioned above. The more influence a person is able to exercise in the role, the higher the role effectiveness is likely to be.

9. Personal Growth

One factor that contributes greatly to role effectiveness is the perception that the role provides the individual with an opportunity to grow and develop. There are many examples of people switching roles primarily because of the opportunity to grow. One head of a training institute accepted a big cut in her salary when she took a new position because she felt that she had nothing more to learn in her previous role. The factor of self-development is very important for role effectiveness. Institutions that are able to plan for the growth of people in their roles have higher role effectiveness and gain a greater contribution from people.

10. Confronting problems

In general, if people in an organization avoid problems or shift them to someone else to solve, their role effectiveness will be low. Confronting problems to find solutions contributes to effectiveness. When people face interpersonal problems and search for solutions their effectiveness is likely to be higher than if they either deny such problems or refer them to their superiors.

You may now like to collect some data about your own organization role and reflect on it by completing the inventory that follows.

A word of caution about the inventory. You will notice that it is not a highly sophisticated instrument and its purpose is quite transparent. This makes it useful only as a guide to your own reflections and I would not recommend its validity to those of you who might be prone to self-delusion! One thing it will do is force you to question some assumptions which you currently make and it may encourage you to clarify some areas of decision-making which you are unclear about.

ROLE EFFECTIVENESS PROFILE: TOOL FOR SELF-ASSESSMENT

The purpose of this inventory is twofold:

1. To provide a structured way of thinking about your current role.
2. To enable positive action to be taken to improve your role effectiveness.

The more honest you attempt to be the better the quality of data you will get back from this inventory. You will probably need to think carefully about the questions rather than make instant responses. Feel free to alter answers if you wish. It is *not* a psychological test.

You will find each question has three sets of statements which you might make about your current role. Tick the one which comes closest to describing your experience of your current role.

You may choose only *one* statement in each set.

1. a My role is very important in this organization; I feel central here.

   b I am doing useful and fairly important work here.

   c Very little importance is given to my role in this organization; I feel peripheral here.

2. a My training and expertise are not fully utilized in my present role.

   b My training and knowledge are not used in my present role.

   c I am able to use my knowledge and training very well here.

3. a I have little freedom in my role; I am only a messenger.

   b I operate according to the directions given to me.

   c I can take initiative and act on my own in my role.

4. a I am doing normal routine work in my role.

   b In my role I am able to use my creativity and do something new.

   c I have no time for creative work in my role.

5. a No one in the organization responds to my ideas and suggestions.

   b I work in close collaboration with some other colleagues.

   c I am alone in my role and have almost no one to consult.

6. a When I need some help none is available.

   b Whenever I have a problem, others help me.

   c I get very hostile responses when I ask for help.

7. a   I do not have the opportunity to contribute to society in my role.

    b   What I am doing in my role is likely to help other organizations or society at large.

    c   I have the opportunity to have some effect on society at large.

8. a   I make some contribution to decisions.

    b   I have no power here.

    c   My advice is accepted by my seniors.

9. a   Some of what I do contributes to my learning.

    b   I am slowly forgetting all that I learned (my professional knowledge).

    c   I have tremendous opportunities for professional growth in my role.

10. a   I dislike being bothered with problems.

    b   When a subordinate brings a problem to me, I help find a solution.

    c   I refer the problem to my boss or to some other person.

11. a   I feel quite central in the organization.

    b   I think I am doing fairly important work.

    c   My role is peripheral to the mainstream of the organization.

12. a   I do not enjoy my role.

    b   I enjoy my role very much.

    c   I enjoy some parts of my role and not others.

13. a I have little freedom in my role.

    b I have a great deal of freedom in my role.

    c I have enough freedom in my role.

14. a I do a good job according to a schedule already decided.

    b I am able to be innovative in my role.

    c I have no opportunity to be innovative and do something creative.

15. a Others in the organization see my role as significant to their work.

    b I am a member of a task force or a committee.

    c I do not work on any committees.

16. a Hostility rather than co-operation is evident here.

    b I experience enough mutual help here.

    c People operate more in isolation here.

17. a I am able to contribute to the company in my role.

    b I am able to serve society at large in my role.

    c I wish I could do some useful work in my role.

18. a I am able to influence relevant decisions.

    b I am sometimes consulted on important matters.

    c I cannot make any independent decisions.

19. a I learn a great deal in my role.

    b I learn a few new things in my role.

    c I am involved in routine or unrelated activities and have learned nothing.

20. a When people bring problems to me, I tend to ask them to work them out themselves.

    b I dislike being bothered with interpersonal conflict.

    c I enjoy solving problems related to my work.

Scoring key

Circle the number corresponding to your response to each of the twenty items. Add up these numbers first for each dimension, then overall, and make a note of the totals. Then compute your Role Effectiveness Index according to the formula given.

Dimension	*Statement*	*Responses*			*Statement*	*Responses*		
		a	b	c		a	b	c
Centrality	1	+2	+1	−1	11	+2	+1	−1
Integration	2	+1	−1	+2	12	−1	+2	+1
Proactivity	3	−1	+1	+2	13	−1	+2	+1
Creativity	4	+1	+2	−1	14	+1	+2	−1
Connections	5	−1	+2	+1	15	+2	+1	−1
Giving and receiving help	6	+1	+2	−1	16	−1	+2	+1
Wider organizational value	7	−1	+2	−1	17	+1	+2	−1
Influence	8	+1	−1	+2	18	+2	+1	−1
Personal growth	9	+1	−1	+2	19	+2	+1	−1
Confronting problems	10	−1	+2	+1	20	+1	−1	+2

Your Total: _____

3	4	3	4

Role effective index

$$\frac{\text{Total score} + 20}{60} \times 100 = \quad \%$$

Interpretation

The scale (-1, $+1$, $+2$) allows a maximum score of $+40$ and a minimum score of -20. Your Role Effectiveness Index represents a percentage of your potential effectiveness in your organization role. A high percentage indicates that you think that in your role you have a great deal of opportunity to be effective.

The ten dimensions of role effectiveness are each measured by two items. Look at each dimension to determine in what areas you perceive yourself as having less than you think you need to be effective. Look for pairs of items for which you have low scores and compare these dimensions. They will provide some basis for reflecting on and discussing possible areas for action.

The result will not provide easy answers but it will point you in the right direction for further reflection and action.

Take for example the statements on Proactivity (3 and 13). These concern the degree of freedom to initiate you feel you have in your job. If you score low on these two, ask yourself whether it is like that because it *must* be like that or is it like that because you *choose* to be like that. If you have consistently tried to initiate and been punished for it, then it is probably a *real constraint*. If however, you haven't tried but 'know' that it would be actively discouraged, it is only an *assumed constraint* because it has never been tested.

Our work life – especially the swampy areas of our roles – is littered with untested assumptions waiting to be tested. Roles do have three quite distinct aspects:

Demands	– things you must do
Constraints	– things you must not do
Choices	– things you may do

Apply the three-aspects test to your low-scoring statements and you may find you have more room for choice and for exercising your role power than you had ever assumed.

EXERTING INFLUENCE – THE STYLES YOU USE

All of us have personal bias when it comes to which style of influencing we prefer to use. Most of us are better at some than others. Sometimes the style we choose can be important in terms of the type of situation we want to change and how ready the individual or system is to change. Roger Harrison has developed a useful classification for identifying influencing styles which identifies four main approaches. They are: assertive persuasion; reward and punishment; common vision; participation and trust.

The four styles are given in more detail below. Basically the broader the spread of styles you can use, the more likely you are to be able to influence effectively in different situations – provided you can recognize which style to use in which situation!

Assertive persuasion

This style is characterized by the use of the power of logic, facts and opinions to persuade others. Individuals who use this style are forward with ideas, proposals and suggestions about what to do and how to do it; they are not afraid to stick their necks out and submit their ideas to the test of others' reactions. They are ingenious in marshalling evidence and arguments in support of the proposals they support, and in rebuttal of those with which they disagree. They are persistent and energetic in persuading others. They often do not listen very well to the points others raise, or they listen only to find weaknesses in the other's position.

Characteristic of this style is an emphasis on logical argument as opposed to appeals to emotions or to the use of power and authority to compel compliance. People who use this style well are usually highly verbal and articulate and participate very actively in discussions and arguments about ideas, plans and proposals. They enjoy the cut and thrust of verbal battles, and even when they are defining an inferior position they may battle away with enthusiasm and determination.

Reward and punishment

This style is characterized by the use of pressure and incentives to control the behaviour of others. This may take the form of offering rewards for compliance and of threatening punishment or deprivation for noncompliance. It may involve the use of naked power, or more indirect and veiled pressures may be exerted through the possession of status, prestige and formal authority. There is liberal use of praise and criticism, approval and disapproval, and of moralistic judgements of right and wrong.

People who use reward and punishment effectively go out of their way to let others know what they want, expect or require of them, and what standards will be used in judging the other's performance. They then follow up to find out what has been done and administer approval and disapproval, praise and blame, rewards and punishments accordingly. They tend to be specific and detailed in communicating their requirements, and they follow up quickly with the positive and negative incentives. Psychologists say that effective use of the style involves much heavier use of praise than of criticism, but many who use this style do not follow this dictum and may be negative more often than positive.

An important process in using reward and punishment is what is called the 'management of contingencies' which means communicating clearly to others what they must do in order to get what they want and to avoid negative consequences. An important aspect of this is bargaining and negotiating, where offers and counter-offers, threats and counter-threats are a big part of the action. Any time one is engaged in letting others know what one will do to or for them *if* they do or don't do such-and-such, one is engaged in 'contingency management'. (For a classic example of contingency management on a grand scale, see Machiavelli's *The Prince*.)

In using both rewards and punishments and assertive persuasion one may agree or disagree with others, and approve of their ideas and actions. The difference is in what backs up the agreement or disagreement, approval or disapproval. In assertive persuasion one may agree or disagree because of one's judgement of the rationality of the other's position, because one thinks it more or less effective, correct, accurate or true. The ultimate appeal is to reason, logic, and reality, to a shared desire to be *efficacious*. In using reward and punishment, on the other hand, the judgement of right and wrong does not depend on rationality. The standard is *external* to the person being judged such as a moral or social standard, a regulation, or a performance standard. It is the compliance or not with this external standard which causes the evaluation of right or wrong, good or bad. The person making the judgement sets himself up as the judge, rather than appealing to a common standard of rationality. (In practice, the best way to tell the difference is to note whether the judgement is given with or without a reason: if it is merely, 'that's right', 'you're wrong', then it's likely the person is setting himself up as judge and administering rewards and punishments. If a reason is given, it's more likely assertive persuasion.)

Common vision

Common vision is a strategy of identifying and articulating a common or shared vision of what the future of an organization, group or activity *could be*, and of strengthening members' beliefs that the desired outcomes *can be achieved* through their individual and collective efforts.

The common vision style involves mobilizing the energy and resources of others through appeals to their hopes, values and aspirations. It also works through activating the feelings of strengths and confidence that are generated by being one of a larger group which shares a common purpose.

Common vision shares with assertive persuasion an emphasis on the ability to present ideas verbally. It differs in that the appeal is not primarily to the intellect, but rather to emotions and values held by the recipient. Further, the attempt is not so much to *inject* energy and enthusiasm into others as it is to *activate* the commitment and strength which are bound up in the others' hopes, aspirations and ideas and to *channel* that energy into work and problem-solving.

Typical of the skills possessed by people who used common vision effectively is the ability to see and to articulate to others the exciting possibilities which exist in an idea or project, and to communicate these possibilities enthusiastically to others. In essence, common vision implies a *future* orientation, and the skilled practitioner uses images and metaphors which kindle excitement about a better future which his hearers may share. He or she also helps them to identify the values, hopes and aspirations which they have in common, and to feel that strength in unity which is found in cohesive groups. The emphasis is on what *we* can accomplish to make a better future for all of *us* if we work *together* to achieve our *common goals and ideals*. Charismatic leaders like Winston Churchill and John F. Kennedy often used common vision, as did others like Hitler, Mussolini and Napoleon. As with all the influence styles, common vision can be equally effective in the pursuit of high ideals or of narrowly selfish ends.

Participation and trust

The efficacy of this style depends on involving the other person(s) in decision-making or problem-solving processes. When the other can be induced to take an active part in making a decision, his or her commitment to carry it out is increased, and the amount of follow-up and supervision required is markedly reduced. He/she actively contributes energy to the work, and the amount of effort required from the influencer is reduced. Thus, where the assertive persuasion and reward and punishment styles can be thought of as 'pushing' the other to do what is required, participation and trust involves drawing the other in, 'pulling' rather than pushing.

In order to involve others actively they should be made to feel that they have resources relevant to the task, that their contributions are received and understood by others, and that others value their efforts. An atmosphere of mutual trust and co-operation is conducive to participation. People are helped to contribute when they believe that others will not belittle or ignore their contributions, and when there is an atmosphere of openness and nondefensiveness. In short, participation is encouraged by receptivity, understanding and openness, and is discouraged by attempting to gain control over others or by competitively trying to win one's own points. Thus the assertive persuasion and reward and punishment styles are in large part incompatible with participation and trust.

Persons who rely a good deal on participation and trust tend to *listen actively*, drawing out contributions from others and showing understanding and appreciation when contributions are forthcoming. They tend to focus on the strengths and positive resources of others. They are willing to give others freedom and personal responsibility in work. They do a lot of building on and extending of the ideas of others, rather than pushing their own proposals, and they are quick to give credit to others for their contributions.

Rather than counter-attacking when their own ideas and proposals are questioned, persons who use this style tend to be open and nondefensive about their own limitations of knowledge and resources. They do not put up a strong front to hide their own weaknesses. By their example they try to create trust and openness in relationships, so that others feel accepted for what they are and do not feel the need to compete for attention and control.

Effective use of the styles

The implications of which patterns we use for influencing are far reaching for our effectiveness in managing change.

The greater the spread across the range of styles, the more chance you have to adapt your behaviour to the needs of the individuals or groups to be influenced. I emphasize that it only gives you the 'chance' because whether you are able or willing to use the appropriate style will depend on other aspects of your interpersonal competence. This competence essentially revolves around three dimensions.

Do you have the behavioural tools to actually deliver the behaviour, whether it be reward and punishment, or participation and trust?

Do you know when to use which skills, depending on your sensitivity to the situation?

Do you have the courage to use the appropriate behaviour when it's needed?

Because influencing is an interactive process the style, or styles, you use need to be appropriate to the needs of those others in the situation. For example, have you ever been to a sales conference where the sales managers are hyped on brass bands, semi-nude women, great sporting personalities, and talk euphorically about winning, divisional prizes and star sales awards?

This is the ultimate common vision approach to influencing. If you score low on common vision, you will find the whole process a complete turn-off. For many sales managers it works because it suits their need style. Give them the logical rational facts of the assertive persuasion approach and they will probably fall asleep.

It can be fun to try and practise using the vocabulary and behaviour of those styles where you score low – but don't think it will be easy. Any one or more of these styles can work for change, provided they are appropriately used.

We have looked at Learning, Power and Influencing, three key tools at your disposal in the implementation process. The better you are at using them, the better your chances of success in changing anything. We now move on to consider the first stage of the change process itself – recognizing the need for change and how to mobilize enough energy and commitment to start making it happen.

SECTION 3

Recognizing the need and mobilizing the commitment to change

Remember those 'Action Man' managers we talked about in the last section? One of their characteristics is their pragmatic, feet on the ground, down to earth approach. On the other hand they are not very good at getting in their helicopter, taking in the whole picture and seeing alternative ways of proceeding. If you recognize yourself as one of these types, make friends with a few reflective managers. At this initial stage in the change process you are going to need them. They are more likely than you are to see possibilities for change and improvement. Like the goldfish having problems recognizing he is in water, it is difficult to see the 'obvious' sometimes. Reflective managers are often better at it. Let's take an example of the real limitations we have as human beings in seeing what's actually in front of us. Take a look at the drawing below and ask yourself what you see. Five shapes perhaps? Now look for the word FLY, (if you're having problems seeing, try putting a border round it). See what I mean? Imagine how much more difficult it is to spot the need to change when you are in the middle of the organizational swamp fighting off alligators.

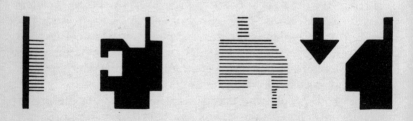

The issue of perception and how to get better at recognizing cues and signals is especially vital at the recognition stage of the change process, and finding ways of keeping the channels as open as possible is a priority. Data collection, reflection and some frameworks with which to work are more important at this stage than action.

Recognition of discrepancies between the internal workings of the organization and the demands of the environment are undoubtedly handled better in some organizations than others. This ability to spot the difference and 'see' what is actually there is crucial to survival and timely change. As a manager you have a key role in this process at whatever level in the organization. The difficulty in spotting necessary changes has to do with a whole range of factors from personal prejudice through to organization culture and history. Knowing that these powerful blocks exist, what can we do to increase our likelihood of receiving important signals?

Use new recruits. They often have the most uncluttered perception of what goes on and why. Their views will be less tainted with organization mythology than yours. Encourage them to give their impressions. Don't make the mistake of waiting until they know their way around; by then their value as an objective viewer will be gone. Use outsiders. I find that I am constantly surprised by the occasional observations of members of my family or friends who know nothing about my work, but see the obvious that I have missed.

The most powerful mechanism I have ever experienced for cutting through conventional wisdom in a company is to put together groups of top managers from different organizations in different sectors – such as engineering, local authority, financial services, construction – and encourage them to ask questions of each other about their businesses and how they are run. These top managers come with no knowledge of each other's business and therefore often ask naive but penetrating questions which insiders would not even think to ask.

Use those people who may be at a lower level in the organization but who operate across the boundary with customers, suppliers or related institutions. They will constantly have access to signals and data which may be important to feed the pattern of data needed to create a recognition of the need to change.

A formal and informal support system has to exist to allow that data to get to you, the decision-maker. Not only does it have to exist but people have to feel encouraged to feed the system.

Even the chief executive does not have the clout to change many things without mobilizing some support for moving to the next stage. So you can imagine how much more difficult it might be for a young salesman to feed in messages from the environment about how the customer sees the company – and get them heard and acted upon, especially if they are contrary to the company's self-image, or managers' self-interest.

CONDITIONS FOR EFFECTIVE RECOGNITION

At this initial stage of the change process there are four necessary conditions for effective recognition of the need to change:

1. Your ability to pick up early cues and signals – especially weak ones.
2. Finding ways of compensating for selective acceptance of data.
3. A willingness to *actively listen* to messages received.
4. A culture in the organization which encourages a flow of signals and information around the system.

1. Big ears for weak signals

This refers to both internal and external signals. It is just as important for an organization to have good internal antennae as it is to have them on its environmental boundary. This is often done by informal line communication, regular meetings, the grapevine, briefings and so on. Very often the best ears in the organization are in certain key non-managerial roles such as waitresses in catering establishments, drivers in distribution and retail, chauffeurs, or porters in hotels, and so on. These people cross boundaries constantly and are a rich source of feedback if listened to. They are the carriers of the rich anecdotal data which is essential for an effective change manager to tap into. These, of course, are in addition to the more formal processes that exist such as exchange of information meetings between companies in the same market place, market surveys, formal consultative processes and so on.

2. Selective acceptance of signals

This is a well researched and common feature of human systems. The protection of a system by refusing to accept unpleasant or hurtful messages is natural and necessary – *to a degree*. The danger is the extent to which this happens. Processes need to be set up to counteract this tendency, such as introducing certain people into discussions who normally wouldn't be there, so that they do not have the same history of what is acceptable and what is not.

One company in which I worked used regularly to invite selected individuals from various parts and levels of the organization to sit in and listen to executive committee meetings. There were certain clear ground rules, such as non-contribution during the meeting, but the individuals were invited to make observations at the end. This unusual process achieved three important ends. It kept the executive committee on its toes to know two junior staff members were listening to their discussions. It also ensured they received some feedback from a non-involved source, albeit heavily filtered due to status differences. Thirdly, it was an excellent way of feeding the grapevine in the organization with data of management's own choosing rather than random and highly speculative data. A few well-established myths about managerial incompetence died in the process!

3. Active listening

This is a difficult concept to get across in words but it is more than 'not talking'. It means not only hearing the messages but working hard to clarify and make sense of them, and then wrestling with the implications for the organization. Once again it is a process which is highly developed in effective managers and which has to be worked hard at. Without doubt the key to active listening – and good quality general management – is the ability to ask good questions without presuming to answer them yourself.

Try it at home one evening. Ask why, how, when, where, what, nod and encourage and, above all, keep your mouth shut and eyes and ears open. You might be surprised just how much you learn. Then try it at work.

4. Flow of information around the organization

This relates closely to the nature of the corporate culture and the extent to which the organization is *fragmented* or *integrated* (discussed in more detail in the section 'Where Are We Now?'). In more fragmented structures information does not flow easily – in fact it is discouraged from doing so as a way of preserving power for those who have the information. In the more integrated system there are usually good formal channels for pushing information up and down, but not always across the organization. This cross-functional or departmental flow of information is an area for special attention since it is here where most information flows fail.

MOBILIZING COMMITMENT

Recognizing is one thing. Energizing people to do something is quite something else. There is only a finite amount of energy available in an organization and if, for example, all that energy is pouring into finding ways of rewarding and reinforcing current behaviour, products and practices, even the most energetic chief executive is going to have an uphill struggle if he sees the need to change things.

The ensuing case highlights admirably how such a problem was tackled, but it must be said that the company in question was fortunate to have a chief executive with a great deal of awareness of organizational process as well as high intuitive skills and very big ears.

The case of International Chemicals

Communication in organizations tends to follow the laws of gravity. It's easier to push down than it is to pump up. For this reason top management often feel isolated, out of touch and uneasy about their understanding of employee concerns and, even more important, their ability to tap the rich vein of ideas lying in the organization.

Described here is a recent and ongoing initiative in a division of an international chemical company to try to overcome this problem in the belief by the chief executive that tapping this resource was essential if the ambitious business strategy of the company was to be achieved.

It highlights the need for a process to be initiated which gains support from a critical mass of people in the organization in order to change something.

The generalized recognition of a need to change was already present but what is of particular significance at this point is just how much energy and management effort was required simply to take the first critical step of turning a 'feeling in the water' by the chief executive that 'things need to change' into a degree of commitment by top management sufficient even to consider action. It is my consistent experience that without this 'front-end' work the change process never retains any real momentum in the face of day-to-day operating pressures and does not stick in the long run.

In addition to the strong belief on the part of the chief executive of this division that tapping ideas and communication was very important, he was also convinced in his own mind that changes needed to take place in the management style of the division although he did not make these views generally known. Several years running the company's Japanese operation had reinforced his views about the importance of commitment and involvement. He was also shrewd enough to appreciate that recognition of the need to change had to be spread beyond just himself. He wanted to find a way of basing changes on real data, but even more importantly he needed the actual collection of that data to begin the process of realization and recognition amongst his more influential senior managers.

The project was launched using an outside consultant as catalyst and was given the title Communication and Performance Project, later to become affectionately known as the CRAP project! It was linked to a statement in the company's business plan outlining very clearly the MD's values and beliefs on the subject: '*To achieve our business plan we need more than just the right products and markets. We need the collective will of every employee, we need teamwork, communicative skills, quality awareness and, above all, total commitment.*'

The overall objective of the project was also linked to the business plan, so it could not simply be seen as an end in itself. Its aim was to contribute to improved business performance by (a) providing high-quality, unfiltered communication from staff to top management about how they saw the business and the way it was managed; (b) enabling management to further its credibility by responding to real, rather than assumed, concerns or issues.

It's not what you do it's the way that you do it

Central to the project was that it should be set up and implemented in a way that involved and obtained commitment from all the people who would be affected. Parallel implementation in action. This meant that a great deal of time and effort was spent in the early stages discussing, presenting and gaining commitment to the project. This was done at every level in the company and the main thrust of this approach was the formation of a steering group of eight people drawn from across departments and levels. Also a line manager was taken out of his job and allocated to manage the project and the initiatives which would flow from it. This symbolic act probably did as much to demonstrate commitment as any other single initiative.

What was done

The vehicle used to achieve the upflow of unfiltered information was a series of twelve meetings, each attended by about twelve people from across the company at all levels from senior management to shop floor. These meetings each lasted three hours and were guided by an outside consultant without any line management involvement. They were called sensing groups because their purpose was just that – to sense the attitudes, views, concerns and ideas of a wide and representative range of staff. On a site of

1000 staff, 150 people were asked to attend such a meeting on a voluntary and randomly selected basis.

Prior to the sensing group meetings the steering group met off site for two days to plan the logistics of group selection and structure and, more important, to agree what specific questions should be asked of the groups. They also considered how the data should be handled afterwards and recommended a timescale and approach for top management response.

The questions asked were as broad as possible to encourage broad and constructive discussion about the company as a whole, rather than focusing on departmental differences.

The process of forming a steering group, taking it away and forming a cohesive, purposeful team on a cross-functional basis was quite deliberate and in itself created a strong commitment to the whole project from the team which then spread somewhat beyond that group.

Sensing group questions

1. Produce a list of:
   (a) Things I like about working at International Chemicals.
   (b) Things I don't like about working here.
2. What could be done to improve working here?
3. What five words would you use to describe:
   (a) The current management style here.
   (b) What you would like it to be.
4. What, if anything, prevents you doing your job to the best of your ability?

The early sensing groups were characterized by a widespread cynicism about the initiative. Another '*flavour of the month*', more '*talk not do*' which '*would probably finish up like quality circles*' (another initiative which foundered a few years previously). It was also noticeable at the start that both the consultant and project manager concerned were unnecessarily anxious about the willingness of shop floor and office employees as well as middle managers to open up and engage in lively, honest discussions about the company and how it was managed.

In the event the quality of data coming out of the groups was generally very high. It was characterized by honesty – in some cases a brutal honesty – and a willingness by the large majority to be constructive rather than treat it as a negative 'griping' session. This degree of commitment and enthusiasm deserved an equal commitment in feedback from management and this was a key feature of the process.

Feedback

It really is not possible to emphasize this point too much. At every stage in the process, opportunity has to be taken to keep feedback flowing. The degree of cynicism is inversely proportional to the volume and quality of feedback travelling through the system.

One small example we experienced during the sensing group process was that about halfway through, a grapevine story filtered back to us that one of the sensing groups had broken up in a fight and had disbanded in disarray. This never actually happened or got near to happening, and was a clear case of lack of information being substituted by fantasy or scaremongering.

In order to reinforce the importance of the feedback process, each group that met received a note within two or three days of their meeting, with a typewritten sheet of their presentation. At the end of the sensing group process a letter was sent out thanking groups for their involvement and restating the timescale of top management discussion and feedback after their consideration of the issues. Each group was also invited back for a brief meeting to discuss and clarify the reactions of top management to the data and the proposed plan of action. Subsequently regular bulletins have been issued to update staff on progress.

Avoiding the 'Report on the Bookshelf' syndrome

We have all experienced the well-written report, full of sensible and important questions for improvement which gradually collects dust on the MD's bookshelf, only to be proudly brought out on special occasions (such as the visits of senior head office personnel or board members!) to evidence the splendid work being done to understand the problems. The sensing group project is a classic contender for this treatment, consisting as it does of a mass of views, opinions, concerns and ideas which cry out for management action in addition to the normal day-to-day running of the business. Everyone agrees broadly that something should be done, but the risk is it's not central to short-run business output.

So how to reduce the likelihood of this happening? The seeds have already been sown. The commitment of the steering group, which is widely based across the organization, would be difficult to turn off – especially when there is also a full-time project manager whose future career development depends on success of the project!

As a result of this three-month process the senior management group of the company are sitting on a great deal of very consistent and clear messages about the way they manage the division and how staff see the business. The news is not all good and there are some uneasy feelings, but undoubtedly the recognition of the need for change and the early stages of commitment are now more widely spread than the chief executive alone. The first important step has been taken. It has been achieved by the MD realizing that the recognition and problem diagnosis stage in the change process is more than a rational, intellectual exercise and that gut-level commitment is needed. The gut-level commitment to move to the vision-building stage cannot be achieved without participation and involvement in the recognition and problem diagnosis process.

That process is now being continued through meetings and discussions aimed at sharing and creating a clearer vision of what might be, and then how to start moving. But the most difficult initial step has been taken.

Sensing groups are only one way of achieving such an end and are not a panacea. The difficult part is prising managers and staff away from short-term tasks for long enough to examine the needs for change. That may well require a tough autocratic approach initially. This must be one of the paradoxes of managing change and the need for early involvement and participation. 'You will be involved whether you like it or not!'

Managing Change and Making It Stick

Whilst recognition of the need to change may well come from the injection of outside data – new manager, new chief executive, a consultant or a set of awful business figures – this in itself is nowhere near enough to mobilize the change process in many organizations, and generally the larger and more bureaucratic the organization, the more difficult it will be.

The energy required to provide the initial kick, to mobilize the critical mass, should not be underestimated.

SECTION 4

Where do we want to get to?
Building a vision for change

What intrigues me especially about this phase of the change process is that there have been a number of occasions recently when chief executives and senior directors have said to me that they do not have a clear vision of what their company will look like in the forseeable future. This, at first, seemed to fly in the face of my firm conviction that a clear vision is vital to moving purposefully towards it. After all, if you don't know when you're going you will probably end up somewhere you don't want to be. However, after a little more probing I was comforted to find that the vision was indeed present, and reasonably clear – but at the level of values and beliefs about what the company *should* be like. This is an important distinction because at this stage in the change process, whilst some of the financial and numerical aspects of the vision can be useful, they are not what concern us here. In fact they can be more of a constraint than a help. We are concerned here with the much more fundamental premise that any lasting vision of the future must be based on strongly held values and beliefs about what should be. This behavioural focus is essential if later, more numerical, aspects of the vision are to bear fruit. In one case of a large UK based engineering company the top management are very sure that they want the company to move from:

Present culture	*Desired culture*
Engineering orientation	Customer orientation
Civil Service CYA* mentality	Results-based mentality
Bureaucratic	Responsive
Centralized	Decentralized
Top–down decisions	Decisions devolved

*CYA = cover your ass

73

This is a clear vision. It is not specific and operationalized, nor is it quantified yet, but at the strategic level it is clear enough. I have found this pattern repeated time after time. Organizations where top people have a clear *generalized* vision of what they want the company to look like, and be like, are running the most successful companies, especially when they are able and willing to communicate it.

Vision-building is not purely a rational process. It needs primarily to engage the left brain and therefore any techniques which can elicit or release creative or intuitive responses is helpful here. I have found the process of using art and collage often useful and powerful. Senior managers initially baulk at this idea but once they have tried it they are amazed at the ideas that can flow from the imagery of a drawing, or a collage. Opposite is an example from a company in the financial services sector. It illustrates how they experience the organization now.

Another interesting approach is to ask directors to work out what animal name best fits their company's current performance, and then to decide what animal would best survive in the current business environment. The engineering company I mentioned earlier decided it needed to be a tiger but was currently a donkey. Some interesting room for cross-breeding there! This can, however, lead to clearer ideas about what key changes need to be made.

The process of vision-building takes place better before diagnosing in any detail the current situation, because the creative processes should be as uncluttered as possible. This is not a time for careful, circumscribed reality. It is a time for flamboyant, creative possibilities and the key ingredients are excitement, energy and enthusiasm. There is plenty of time later to connect back with pragmatism. What follows is a case example of how one company began to set about this vision-building process with a particular emphasis on examining the need to change certain aspects of its organization culture.

CREATING A VISION FOR THE FUTURE – A CASE STUDY

This case concerns an already successful growth company in the unit-linked insurance sector.

The company decided to take positive steps to manage its own

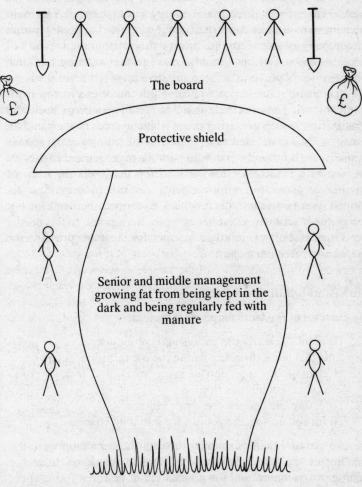

The board

Protective shield

Senior and middle management
growing fat from being kept in the
dark and being regularly fed with
manure

culture by choosing those aspects of the culture it wanted to retain
and finding ways of losing the less favourable aspects. The company, because of its rapid growth and the acquisition of diverse new
managerial talent, felt it was losing some of its original culture of
youthful, entrepreneurial drive and was entering a period of uncertainty and fragmentation. The company still had well-defined
quantitative business objectives but was becoming less clear about

75

how these objectives could be achieved. The recognition of the need to change was present and energy was mobilized. Top management were already concerned about what was happening within the company in spite of continuing growth and profitability, and had therefore embarked on a middle management training initiative some two years previously. This initiative involved several stages. The diagnostic stage began with in-depth interviews at top management level. These were designed to identify concerns about the organization as well as clarifying the training needs of their middle managers. It was decided as a result that the training programmes should be used not only to develop middle management capability but also as a vehicle for feedback to top managers on areas of potential organization improvement. As the programmes developed over two years, this feedback confirmed the need for top management action in a number of areas. In response to this need a two-day workshop was jointly developed for the managing director and the top fifteen managers.

The Vision-building workshop

The purpose of the workshop was threefold:

1. To identify clearly the causes and consequences of the problems that were surfacing within the organization, such as lack of clear policy direction in some areas, and lack of cross-functional communication.
2. To define the desired corporate culture.
3. To formulate specific actions for initiating change.

The two parallel themes running through the workshop were the handling of the issues fed back by middle managers from the training programmes, and the application of research frameworks on corporate cultures to the company's own situation. These were dealt with alternately and in parallel as each provided data and ideas for handling the other. It was known that the vague area of company culture was a difficult one for senior managers to handle and therefore a logical sequence was developed for working.

Workshop Structure

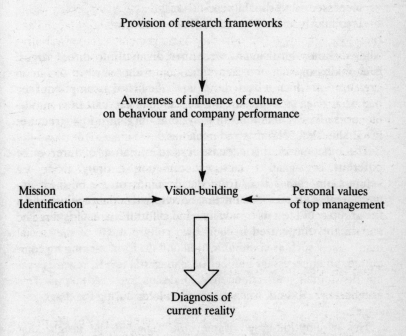

Provision of research frameworks

↓

Awareness of influence of culture
on behaviour and company performance

↓

Mission → Vision-building ← Personal values
Identification   of top management

⇓

Diagnosis of
current reality

The workshop began with a framework concerning the examination of managerial values and assumptions. This was done by providing the participants with three sets of assumptions relating to people at work.

1. *Rational-economic man* is:
   Primarily motivated by economic interests
   Essentially passive
   Without self-control and self-discipline
   Rational

2. *Social man* is:
   Basically motivated by social needs and finds his sense of identity through relationships
   More responsive to the social pressures of his peer groups than to the incentive and control of management

3. *Self-actualizing man*
   Seeks autonomy and independence
   Needs to use his capabilities and skills
   Is primarily self-motivated and has self-control

The workshop participants were then divided into three groups, each taking one set of assumptions, and were asked to design an organization which reflected the particular set of assumptions they had been given. Specifically, these focused on such areas as corporate objectives, communication systems, organization structure, leadership style, rewards and penalties.

The outcome of this exercise was the creation of three quite different organization cultures stemming entirely from the assumptions rather than from the demands of the business environment. This provided the first benchmark of data against which the group could test its own values and cultural characteristics. The participants recognized in their own culture many of the 'social man' values such as communication and decision-making by committee, an unnecessary number of managerial levels, rewards evenly distributed and a tendency to discourage risk-taking. This insight was recorded, to be returned to later during the diagnostic stage.

This assumption-based framework triggered the insight that many key decisions about a company's operation are based entirely on the underlying values and assumptions of managers and that unless they are conscious of these, the direction of the business may well be influenced more by internal values than the requirements of the competitive environment. A dangerous practice, often seen when 'closed system' mentalities are around.

The next step was to provide a framework for understanding and categorizing corporate culture, for which the Deal and Kennedy classification of four company types was used.

Key elements in Corporate Culture

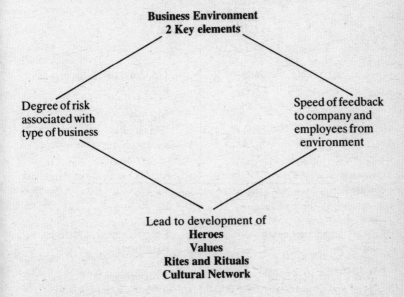

This further enabled the group members to relate their own experience to the frameworks presented, and in this way to acquire a language with which to describe their own company's current culture.

Vision-building

We were now ready to take a step into the future and begin the vision-building process. Three groups were each asked to consider, and agree upon, 'the five characteristics which *you believe must be central values* in the future company culture if it is to continue as a successful business enterprise'.

Four 'pure' cultural types

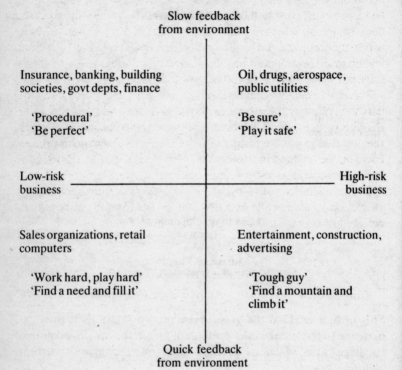

Slow feedback
from environment

Insurance, banking, building
societies, govt depts, finance

'Procedural'
'Be perfect'

Oil, drugs, aerospace,
public utilities

'Be sure'
'Play it safe'

Low-risk
business

High-risk
business

Sales organizations, retail
computers

'Work hard, play hard'
'Find a need and fill it'

Entertainment, construction,
advertising

'Tough guy'
'Find a mountain and
climb it'

Quick feedback
from environment

The following key words and phrases resulted from this task:

Firm but fair
Success
Hard work and commitment
Good surroundings
Frank, constructive and purposeful
Reactive
Personal commitment

It became clear that whilst the lengthy and sometimes difficult discussions which followed ran the risk of being bland, over-general and platitudinous, they did provide some clear pointers about what should be valued in the company. If, for example 'hard work' is valued per se, does that mean regardless of quality of results? This raised fierce debate within the group about what *really* should be rewarded – hard work and loyalty or achievement of results? It, and other debates like it, at this stage paved the way for the second and crucial stage in vision-building.

The chief executive and his three executive directors took away the data generated by the groups to decide what they now felt should be the four or five central values and culture characteristics upon which they wanted to pin the company's future success. Whilst this process could not be finalized in a few hours, what emerged from a short, two-hour meeting was some very clear, albeit initial, statements of culture.

First of all the executive group restated in clear, unambiguous terms its mission statement and *how* they wanted the company to behave in achieving this.

Core mission and required culture

Core Mission:	To dominate the group's* insurance and unit trust customer base
'Required Culture' Statement	— Market oriented
	— Achievement oriented
	— Achievement oriented
	— Executive directors to lay down policy matters
	— Company to be approachable (internal and external)
	— Fun
	— High-quality working environment

---

*This refers to the financial services group of which this company is part.

This was then fed back to senior managers for discussion, under-standing and clarification.

This was only a beginning, and certainly not a good enough basis on which to construct an operating plan. However, in terms of the *process*, there was already a great deal more understanding and the beginnings of a commitment to some basic values and ideas about the company's future. A good foundation had been laid.

It was now time to turn to an analysis of the current culture and organization. What better way than to start with the senior man-agers and examine *their* behaviour, values and ways of working. We already had plenty of concrete experience of that from the work-shop itself.

Diagnosis of current situations

We wanted to demonstrate that corporate culture is transmitted to employees by the behaviour of, and the examples set by, their senior executives rather than by what they say in newspapers and annual reports. In order to do this we returned to diagnosis of the current culture and asked the question: 'What is the culture of *this* group as expressed by its behaviours and rituals during this work-shop so far?'

The following five themes emerged as the most consistently observed:

— Individuals want to see which way the wind will blow before committing themselves

— Ritual disagreement

— Concentration on unnecessary detail

— Avoidance of conflict

— Avoidance of decision-making

In addition, the consultants observed a number of behaviours which were characteristic of the group. The two most important of these were 'little or no building on comments and ideas' and 'consistent evidence of frustration which remained unexpressed'. What we, and the group, had described here as characteristic of senior management behaviour during the workshop began to mirror the issues raised by their middle managers about the present organization. This reinforced the uncomfortable reality that the organization is a reflection of the behaviour of its top executives. So the recognition of the need to change was further taking shape in quite concrete form.

The next step was to concentrate on systematically identifying the current company culture. To do this we used a diagnostic questionnaire (developed with one of the senior managers prior to the workshop) about six other companies which were well known to the managers. This would provide a comparative analysis. These companies were selected from finance, retail and manufacturing sectors. This process, using a checklist of forty paired culture characteristics, introduced the group to the type of analysis to be used on their own company. They then individually completed a questionnaire which concentrated on organization, marketing and management aspects of the company. Then they established the strongly positive and strongly negative dimensions which were commonly perceived.

The outcome of this process was one clearly identified strength – namely a positive attitude to market oriented product development, and three problem areas – namely too many layers in the organization, too much centralized control, too little differentiation in rewards.

So by the second evening – twenty-four hours into the workshop – we were at the point of focusing specifically on the current company culture, having already begun to draw a picture of how we would like it to look in the future.

In addition, a summary of interview data collected two years previously from top managers by the consultants was presented to remind the group of key words used to describe the company at that time. There were some remarkable similarities between the themes mentioned then and the data being generated now.

A look at the sample below shows that even two years ago certain inconsistencies in the culture were present (e.g. 'open' *vs.* 'not approachable' or – 'aggressive' *vs.* 'friendly'), which many companies might ignore but which in this company's case had led them to take the difficult step of encouraging middle management

Sample of interview data verbatim comments (from original data – two years previously)

Description of Organization Climate	Describe Company as a Person	Company Perceived Strengths (+) and Weaknesses (−)
Top management not approachable	Young confident	+ Committed people
	Aggressive	+ Adaptable
Feeling of lost youth	Friendly	− Empire building
Dynamic	Adolescent	− Haphazard Decision-making
Rank and status important	Gangling youth	
	Frenetic	− Too many meetings
Consultative	Ambivalent	− Too much consensus
Fast pace	Trusting	− Steep hierarchy
Wide range of styles		
Open		

to voice their concerns about the way the company was operating and of setting up a workshop to identify positive actions which could be taken by senior management. The information from the original senior management interviews, the feedback from middle management and the data from the workshop discussions were worked on in small groups and presented in plenary session. The major issues identified can be summarized as follows:

— Lack of clarity about roles, responsibilities and authorities

— Strong functional infrastructure rather than business-related structure

— Inadequate lateral communication

— Slow decision-making

— Need to prioritize increasing volume of work more effectively

— Top management too distant

Making it happen

At this point each of the executive directors (there were four, including the MD) were asked to lead a group in the task of identifying the first steps that needed to be taken in order to begin to move from the current situation to the ideal vision. Each group took two areas and came up with a list of action steps, both immediate and longer term, which could be taken.

Samples of 'How to make it happen' ideas

Market Orientation

Posters

Create heroes

Bulletins on results

Market orientation sessions

Pay staff commission for selling products

Display stands

Increase direct feedback from customers

Non-marketing people to meet customers

Approachability

Plain language documents

'Help' desk introduced

Change reception area

More visible management

Improve lateral communication

Executive Directors' Policy Direction

Focus on *what* not *how*

Define ground rules of consultation

Clarify responsibility boundaries

Push for upward communication

High-quality Environment

Maintain current image/quality

Review work space, open plan

Catering

Sports, social facilities

Achievement Oriented

Clear targets

Fun

'Seriousness of purpose with levity of approach'

Short timescales	Increase trust
Milestones set up	Reduce bureaucracy and levels, therefore frustration
Recognize and reward	Individual and small group motivation
Remunerate on merit	Clearer responsibilities will help

The data generated at the vision stage is very general – but it has to be. If it is too specific it can stifle development; it should be strategically clear only. From there on the outcome will depend on the effective management of the process by the top and middle managers. There is a long way to go yet. Only time will tell.

One thing is sure, however. Without the messy process of working through vision-building and articulating the sort of company top management want it to be, effective change will probably never happen.

The next stage is to embark on the process of diagnosing the current culture and climate in more detail so that action strategies can be developed.

This particular vision-building case focused on changing aspects of culture, but the vision could equally well be more broadly based in terms of potential growth size, nature of products, market share and so on. Either way, having gone through the vision-building process we are in a much stronger position to take a good hard look at where we stand now.

SECTION 5

Where are we now?

In this section we will explore a number of areas which I have found especially useful as anchors in the organization sea. The problem in diagnosing anything is knowing where to start and what yardsticks to use. Being perceptive and seeing signals is one thing but knowing what they mean is quite something else.

In terms of the learning model used earlier we now have more than enough data. We now need to move into a reflecting mode with some good frameworks and theories to help us understand what we see and turn it into appropriate action. A general manager I am working with explained to me recently that his organization works on the basis of what he calls 'conspiracy theory'. He means that if he allowed more of his senior subordinates to meet together too frequently they would begin plotting against him and the organization. He therefore keeps them very busy and very separated from each other. A feudal theory perhaps, but a theory nonetheless, and one which he lives by. Many 'theories' like this are locked up in common clichés about organizations – 'small is beautiful', 'tidy desks mean tidy minds' and so on.

For our purposes here we need some rather more robust concepts which still have practical value. The concepts we shall use are:

* Stages of organizational development
* Managing organizational crises
* Open systems theory
* Managing the emotional processes
* Readiness to change

STAGES OF ORGANIZATIONAL DEVELOPMENT

In order to improve our understanding of the management of change, the growth and development of the organization is a helpful focus. It enables us to view the massive amount of information available in a systematic and logical fashion.

The developmental approach establishes a useful framework within which to co-ordinate knowledge, provides direction and has explanatory and predictive value. More importantly, I have found it of enormous practical value when working with managers trying to decide where to start and what to do. It provides a sound basis for both looking at where we are now as well as a possible future vision of where we want to be. Although it was not used in the case quoted in the previous section, a look at the data will clearly show symptoms of 'transition behaviour', suggesting the company is at a crisis point in its development. The developmental approach looks at the evolution of an organization, with particular reference to the phases through which it passes and the forces at work governing its growth and development.

The main contributors to this developmental approach are Blake, Avis & Mouton, Lievegoed, and Greiner.

In 1966 Blake, Avis & Mouton published their book *Corporate Darwinism* in which they identified phases in the evolution of the modern corporation and described their approach as 'a strategy of thinking which has proved uncommonly useful for understanding the forces which bring about change in an orderly and predictable way'. They identify six stages in the evolution of the modern corporation:

1. The food-gathering family
2. The food-producing village
3. Commercialization of economic life
4. The entrepreneurial corporation
5. The mechanistic corporation
6. The dynamic corporation

In Holland, at much the same time, B.C.J. Lievegoed, a medical man with a sociological bent, and Professor of Social Pedagogy at the Rotterdam School of Economics, was finding a developmental approach to the study of organizational growth of considerable value and had established a consulting organization, the N.P.I., to implement this approach in helping industrial concerns with their organizational problems.

Lievegoed identifies three phases in the development of modern organizations, which he calls:

1. The pioneer phase
2. The phase of differentiation
3. The phase of integration

These are very similar to the stages outlined by Blake, Avis & Mouton though Lievegoed approaches them through systems theory. He constructs what he calls 'a developmental model' in which the following 'laws' can be discerned:

— Development is principally discontinuous.

— Development occurs in time in a series of stages.

— Within each stage a system appears which has a structure characteristic of that stage.

— Within this system variables and sub-systems appear of which one is dominant.

— In a following stage the structure differs from the previous one in that it has a higher degree of complexity and differentiation.

— The new stage has a new dominant sub-system. This does not lead to a process of addition but to a shifting of all the relationships within the system.

— Development is not reversible.

Lievegoed makes a clear distinction between growth and development. Growth he defines as 'an increase in size, without a change of structure'. Development involves a change in structure, usually accompanied by periods of crisis or turbulence.

This distinction between growth and development is implicit in Greiner's model as well. Greiner uses the term 'evolution' to describe 'the quieter periods' in the growth of an organization, but says that 'smooth evolution' is not inevitable, nor can it be assumed that 'organizational growth is linear'. There are periods of turbulence when 'traditional management practices which were appropriate for a smaller size and earlier time' have to change. He uses the term *revolution* to describe 'those periods of substantial turmoil in organization life'. The organization advances through evolutionary and revolutionary phases.

Greiner lists five key dimensions for his model of organization developments:

1. Age of the organization
2. Size of the organization
3. Stages of evolution
4. Stages of revolution
5. Growth rate of the industry

On the basis of these dimensions he constructs a model of organization development involving five phases of evolution. This model is of particular practical value when looking at change in organizations.

Phase 1   Creativity
Phase 2   Direction
Phase 3   Delegation
Phase 4   Co-ordination
Phase 5   Collaboration

The transition from one evolutionary stage to the next is marked by a period of turmoil, revolution or crisis which warrants further examination. The understanding and effective management of these crises is a key to the management of change. The word 'crisis', incidentally, derives from the Chinese and translates literally as 'dangerous opportunity'. This emphasizes not only the risks of crisis but the positive outcomes which can derive from it – a good point to remember in such situations in order to maintain a positive bias for action.

So what are the likely organizational crises which we might encounter in the life of an organization at each of these evolutionary stages?

THE FIVE PHASES OF GROWTH AND CRISIS

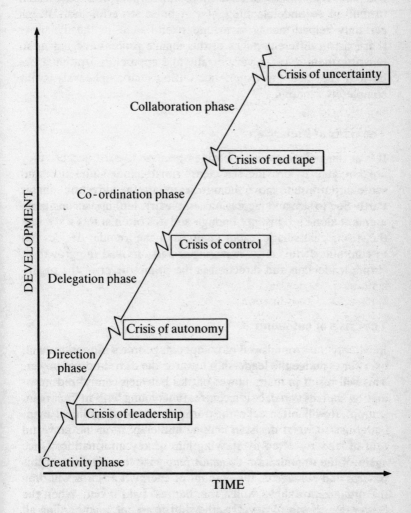

This is a particularly good framework for diagnosis because it has a sequential logic which helps to de-confuse organizational complexity. This is also a danger in that there is a temptation to believe that this relatively simple linear model actually represents time reality. No model can reflect the shadings, subtleties and complexities of organizational life but, provided we accept it as a useful aid to understanding, it can be a powerful tool. It has certainly helped managers to understand some of the dynamics that exist at different stages of the change process and begins to reassure them that the very erratic and apparently irrational behaviour they see and experience during major upheavals is not completely random.

The crisis of leadership

It is at this point that many businesses cease to exist because they are not able to provide the clear, single-minded direction and sense of purpose to move them forward into the 'direction' phase. Partly due to size and increasing complexity, enthusiasm and commitment alone are just not enough and it is often at this stage that the strong charismatic leader emerges or the founder decides not to continue. If this crisis is managed and survived the growth of strong leadership and direction is the prime driver of the organization.

The crisis of autonomy

Inevitably the groundswell of competent people's aspirations will, over time, nudge the leadership towards the devolution of power. This will result in many power battles between centralized information sources and decision centres, and young bulls in the organization. It will often take the form of elaborate political manoeuvrings to wrest decision-making authority from the powerful central leader – often by starving him of key information. Once again, if the organization does not recognize the existence of this process and manage it, the amount of energy it absorbs will drag the organization down whilst the 'barons' fight it out. When the power does begin to devolve, the shift from one man holding all the strings to a broad-based decision-making structure is often quite dramatic. So much so that over time the organization becomes increasingly fragmented and unco-ordinated. This often becomes apparent in fairly dramatic ways, such as loss of profits, orders and growth, due to unplanned development and a lack of overall strategy. Another crisis looms.

The crisis of control

It is at this point that the bureaucratic machine begins to establish itself and the move towards co-ordination takes place. Power and decisions are still devolved but in a proceduralized, systematic and regulated way. Accountability becomes a byword for the first time. Probably at this point the organization begins to consider strategic planning of some sort and a platform of systems and policies will be developed to regulate the behaviour of managers and staff at all levels. At the point when this all threatens to stifle the development and initiatives of the organization the next seeds of crisis are sown.

The crisis of red tape

Here the options are legion. There are many ways to develop. Somehow the organization must find a way of freeing itself from the clutter of rules and regulations that bind it so that it can once again attack its markets and competitors – or simply achieve its mission more effectively. The great risk of this crisis is that it is a very thin line between developing a more participative, collaborative system and anarchy. Co-ordination is needed but with a great deal more flexibility than previously.

The crisis of uncertainty

Greiner was unsure back in 1972 about the exact nature of the next crisis. It is interesting to speculate what it may be. My own experience suggests that what happens at the end of the collaboration stage is that there is an increasing confusion about the core mission of the organization which requires some form of return to strong, clear leadership. Whether the leadership can be of the same single-minded, power-oriented type as existed initially seems very unlikely, but there is certainly a need for either an individual or – more likely – a small, powerful team to lead the organization strongly and to provide a clear, strong sense of purpose and mission. It is quite possible that the mission will involve breaking up the organization into smaller sub-units which have autonomy within a clear overall framework and culture. Perhaps 'Crisis of Uncertainty' sums up this stage best.

THE MANAGEMENT OF CRISIS

The crises themselves can often be protracted periods of considerable turbulence over many years or they can slip past almost unnoticed by the organization members. This will to some extent be determined by how sensitively the crisis is managed – or indeed whether it is even recognized by top managers.

There are quite clear stages of crises. Original work by psychologists and psychiatrists in the area of personal crisis management such as bereavement or divorce has shown consistent patterns of behaviour through which an individual passes. This can also be applied to organizations in crisis.

The four phases of crisis are: shock; defensive retreat; reality acceptance; adaptation and growth.

It is of course possible to become locked in any one of these phases for considerable periods of time and in such cases behaviour becomes ritualistic and repetitive. For example, a leader who has lost his power base may continue in the defensive retreat stage for a long time, unable to accept the changed reality and behaving as if he still had the power. If this continues he will alienate himself further and further from those around him until he is removed completely from the scene. This can sometimes be seen in political dictatorships, a recent example being President Marcos of the Philippines.

I recently spent time with a senior manager in a very large corporation which has been experiencing its crisis of red tape. This man has for years, as a central staff man, held considerable decision-making power. He is now suddenly left with none of that power because it has been given out to regional directors. He has been truly 'shell-shocked' for between six and twelve months and now describes himself as wounded but actively looking for a new role. He is just moving tentatively into the adaptation and growth stage after a painful journey through reality acceptance. Some people never make it. I meet many managers at quite senior levels in organizations who talk about little else but the importance of their own role and status. This is often a signal that they are, at least partly, trapped in the defensive retreat stage of some career or organizational crisis. Energy is being used up in justifying where and what they are, rather than where they might go. Helping managers come through this to release positive energy for the organization is a critical managerial task of crisis management. It requires guts, care and, often, a lot of patience.

This crisis model can be applied to the organization's behaviour, and the chart which follows (based on work by Fink and Bink) applies it to various key aspects of organizational functioning.

If you are ever faced with bizarre, irrational behaviour by an organization, have a look at the chart shown here and you may well get more insight into what is happening and why. It lists in some detail the sort of behaviour you can expect to find at various stages of crisis in the organization.

AN OPEN SYSTEMS VIEW OF ORGANIZATIONS

Open systems theory is useful for the understanding of change because it helps us determine where to put our limited energy to work when all hell is let loose. Remember the 'action man' trap! You may be tempted to skip this section if you are one of those. Why not grit your teeth and give it a try? Its special utility as a theory is that it can apply to any social system, from two people to a whole organization. Every supervisor or manager at whatever level, manages an open system.

You will know this from your own experience when you have just managed to get your own department on an even keel as far as job grades or salary levels are concerned and suddenly some manager in a totally unrelated department to yours (as far as work is concerned) manages to get his people upgraded or his establishment figures increased. You soon find out how 'unrelated' your two departments are! That's open systems theory at work.

There are some important features to bear in mind about open systems:

Phases of organizational crisis

PHASE	Interpersonal relations	Intergroup relations	Communication	Leadership and decision-making	Problem-handling	Planning and goal-setting	Structure
Shock	Fragmented	Disconnected	Random	Paralysed	None	Dormant	Chaotic
Defensive retreat	Protective cohesion	Alienated	Ritualized	Autocratic	Mechanistic	Expedient	Traditional
Reality acceptance	Confrontation (supportive)	Mutuality	Searching	Participative	Explorative	Synthesizing	Experimenting
Adaptation and change (growth)	Interdependent	Coordinated	Authentic congruent	Task-centred	Flexible	Exhaustive and integrative	Organic

— *Inputs* are obtained from outside the system. For an individual human being, the inputs are food, air, heat and information; for an organization they are information, energy, raw materials, people, knowledge, etc.

— *Outputs* are delivered to the environment. For an individual human being, the outputs are motion, heat, waste, ideas and information; for an organization they are added value information, energy and/or some physical product, profit.

— The '*creative transformation*' which the system performs on inputs to produce outputs. The creative transformations for an individual include converting food to energy, information into ideas or new kinds of information; for an organization they include the processes by which its products or services are created from raw materials – manufacturing processes as well as administrative and control processes.

— *Feedback* from the environment on the effects created by the outputs. For the individual, feedback includes the observation of a change created by a physical act, or the perception of the effect of one's communication on another person. For an organization, feedback may be the volume of sales which indicates how desirable the product is, the number of applicants for a job opening, the media or public view of the organization.

— A *maintenance envelope* which protects the system from unwanted inputs from the environment. For a human being, the envelope includes one's skin and the selective perception which protects us from too many, or unwanted, stimuli; for organizations, the envelope consists of barriers such as reception areas and security checks concerning recruitment or company secrets, policies and procedures and many other regulatory aspects of the organization. If overdone, this may block feedback. At the individual level, the famous 'open door policy' adopted by many managers is a good example of managing the maintenance envelope or 'boundary' of one's personal system. It recognizes the need to keep channels open but if overdone causes the manager to become overloaded and ineffective.

The *nature* of the system affects what it does proficiently and what it does poorly. For example, if Ashridge Management College decided to enter the motor manufacturing business, which is very different from the current business of the organization, there would be a long learning period during which many inefficient and unsuccessful efforts would be undertaken. Similarly, a given individual may be poorly suited by his nature to playing a musical instrument and well suited to doing engineering work; his performance capability (transformation processes) in each of these fields would be quite different. Another example of this is the extent to which organizations where specialist technical or scientific skills are valued have problems managing themselves unless they recognize the need to recruit and/or develop managerial capability as well.

— The *total energy* available in a system at any given moment is *finite*, and the more of that energy that goes into one kind of function, the less is available for other functions. For example, if an organization is currently engaged in producing the final stages of development of a piece of equipment on a very tight schedule for delivery to a customer, it is not likely to have much energy available for listening to a product development division that wants to consider investing in a new product. Similarly, if an individual is currently engaged in answering many questions from his boss about the status of a current project, it is not likely that he has a great deal of energy available for working on that project. New projects are especially vulnerable to this interference from top management and the project manager has to manage his boundary very carefully. This is especially relevant to change situations since any change requires a lot of energy, and choices need to be made about where to expend it.

— *Tendency to maintain the status quo* is a feature of all open systems since they are essentially conservative in nature and therefore resisting change of any significance will be a natural and expected response.

The Organisation as an open system

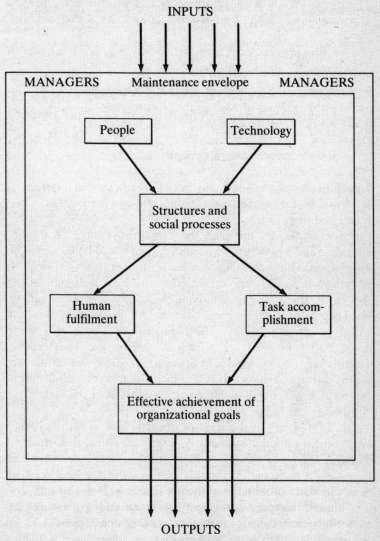

Open systems and change

There are, then, a number of key factors which quickly become apparent about changing any system if one looks at such a model.

— Changing the people, or their behaviour, is not necessarily enough – even at the top.

— Altering the technology alone is not enough.

— Modifying structures, decision-making or reward processes alone is not enough.

— Resistance will naturally occur.

To achieve a visible shift of any lasting significance in a system, at least two of the interacting variables have to be tackled – preferably all three.

For example, let me take the common example of training courses. Send a manager on a training course and he increases his awareness, skill and enthusiasm for trying out new behaviour. If he returns to an organization with the same basic technologies and the same structure, problem-handling, decision-making and reward processes, this new piece of input into the people system will wither away very quickly. The biological analogy is also useful here. Social as well as biological systems are conservative, evolutionary and prefer not to move too far from the status quo. So any attempt to change direction by influencing one small part of that system will come under great pressure from the status quo 'antibodies', as happens in transplant surgery.

This also occurs at the level of departmental systems within a larger organizational system. A keen, thrusting departmental manager can make changes within his sub-system but he must be very careful to recognize that his is an *open* system and what he does will affect other parts of the organization. If not he will soon find himself bumping up against subtle but strong pressures for conformity from colleagues, bosses or other departments.

I experienced this when working on some job redesign activities where we changed levels of responsibilities of supervisors to enable them to make decisions that managers had previously made. Whilst the changes were made in certain parts of the organization only, there were great difficulties when supervisors began phoning managers in the 'unchanged' departments. These managers insisted on the decision coming from counterpart managers rather than supervisors. This reaction from the sub-system's 'environment' created problems for some time until the manager of the 'change target' system took active steps to manage his boundary with his colleagues in other departments.

The difference between 'knowing it' and 'behaving it'

Intellectually it is common for managers to accept as obvious the idea of open systems that interact with their environment and not many would argue with the sense of it. The problem is that time and again *behaviour* is not consistent with this view. There are many examples of this, probably the most topical and commonly experienced being that of the data processing department in many companies. The irony is that in their technical work DP departments understand and use the open system concept extremely well but are often unable to apply it to their interaction with their user environment. I know of one company where the DP department carries out a feasibility study with the user then retreats into a 'black box' for months on end while the 'technical development' takes place. This is a wonderfully rational process but totally ignores the reality that social and people systems exist and have needs. Lo and behold, when the technical solution arrives, either the needs have changed or attitudes have hardened and resistance is encountered. As one user manager said to me, 'Our technical people are brilliant. They produce outstanding technical solutions which never quite seem to match the business problems we have.' This is a very simplified example of the cost of ignoring social processes in the system and, more importantly, demonstrates a lack of awareness of the consequences of closing off regular contact with users. This fairly typical behaviour between departments in an organization illustrates well the way in which behaviour patterns reflect the 'closed system' view of organizations. Keeping channels open is vital, especially when there is no specific problem to discuss. If you don't – there will be soon enough!

Evolution or revolution

A characteristic of open systems, whether animal, human or organizational, is that they tend to develop in an evolutionary and incremental way rather than in a revolutionary way.

Organizations are sometimes exceptions to this principle, because they do occasionally suffer severe jolts triggered either from inside or outside. One thing an organization can do which human systems cannot is to grow by acquisition, for example, and this often causes major trauma to both systems concerned, especially if the nature of open systems is not fully understood.

Change of an incremental, adapting, modifying nature is the order of the day for most of the time in organizations and, whilst we shall look at some examples of managing major upheaval, for the most part it is sensible to focus on the change process as most of us will experience it and be expected to manage it. It is, perhaps, less exciting and dramatic but in the end organizations succeed largely on how well they adapt and grow through developmental and incremental change rather than how often they cope with major earthquakes.

Sadler and Barry's framework for analysis of organization development is based on the open systems view of organization and suggests three key dimensions important to the functioning of the organization: the degree of control exercised by management; the degree of integration of activities and functions in the system; the 'fit' between these interacting dimensions and the type of environment within which the system is operating. This can then be seen as a four quadrant model with each quadrant having distinctive characteristics. Once there is a clear understanding of where the organization is operating, it is then possible to see whether this fits the environment. For example, if a hi-tech company in the software development field is operating with high functional integration and high managerial control, in other words bureaucratically, it will have problems because its business environment is fast-moving, turbulent and competitive. The fit is wrong and the system won't survive. The model was not intended to indicate stages of development, but in using it over the years and adding to it data from Roger Harrison on organization ideology and Charles Handy on organizational styles, it becomes clear that the quadrant characteristics do almost invariably appear in a developmental sequence which fits Lievegoed's laws of development.

This framework is worthy of mention because it does seem consistently to fit managers' experience of their real world and also helps to create a basis for thinking about directions for change. Peter Smith, at Ashridge, has developed an instrument for assessing the current whereabouts of an organization on this model which I have found extremely valuable as a starting point for dialogue with senior managers about their organization. It is reproduced here, so that you can try it for yourself as a way of diagnosing your organization or department.

A word of interpretation. One person's perception will hardly be of any predictive value, but if, for example, a reasonable random percentage of your managers see the organization in the same way, this is very significant, and *factual*, data. If they see it that way they will behave accordingly and so, probably, will many others. It will almost always point you in the right direction.

ORGANIZATIONAL PROFILE: TOOL FOR ASSESSMENT

How to complete the inventory

Here are some statements about certain aspects of your present work organization and your experience of it.

Please read each statement carefully and decide whether you *agree* or *disagree* with the statement in terms of your own work experience, then tick the appropriate box alongside. You may complete it about your organization *or* a division of it, but whatever level you choose – be consistent throughout.

There are no right or wrong answers and this is not a test of ability or intelligence. So work steadily through it, and be frank, please.

Managing Change and Making It Stick

1. Everyone in the organization generally knows what contribution he makes to the whole. ☐ ☐

2. Management is not very approachable. ☐ ☐

3. Loyalty to one's own department tends to come first. ☐ ☐

4. Everyone is pleased when the company is successful. ☐ ☐

5. People spend a lot of time blaming others for their own mistakes. ☐ ☐

6. I generally know where to go when I want help. ☐ ☐

7. They tell us we are here to carry out instructions. ☐ ☐

8. I am proud of the success of my company. ☐ ☐

9. Decisions always seem to come down from the top. ☐ ☐

10. There seems to be quite a lot of friction and not much co-operation between departments. ☐ ☐

11. Management encourages superiors to discuss new proposals with their subordinates. ☐ ☐

12. People normally consider the effect of their actions upon the whole organization. ☐ ☐

13. The only way we learn of changes is by the grapevine. ☐ ☐

14. It is not uncommon here to get conflicting orders and instructions. ☐ ☐

15. On the whole, people do not feel very free to speak their minds. ☐ ☐

	agree	disagree
16. People seem to prefer to get on with the job by themselves.	☐	☐
17. One's job depends not so much on titles or activities but on what sort of position you can carve out for yourself.	☐	☐
18. Normally staff are expected to accept orders without question.	☐	☐
19. People in the organization only get together when there is a crisis.	☐	☐
20. Managers place value on the opinions of subordinates.	☐	☐
21. In my job, I am rather unclear about what goes on in other functions.	☐	☐
22. I don't think many people below senior management really understand the organization's objectives.	☐	☐
23. I often find it difficult to know who to approach for information.	☐	☐
24. Managers seem more concerned about the narrow interest of their department rather than wider company objectives.	☐	☐
25. Management is pretty intolerant of error and is not very good at listening to explanations.	☐	☐
26. On the whole, communication in the company seems to be pretty full and free.	☐	☐
27. In our company, subordinates are not afraid to say what they think.	☐	☐
28. Wider participation in management is seen as a desirable objective by the organization.	☐	☐

agree   disagree

29. All too often no one knows what his counterpart in another part of the organization is doing about things that affect them both.

☐   ☐

30. Managers tend to use their power to coerce subordinates.

☐   ☐

31. In our company, I think subordinates exercise quite a lot of influence on their bosses.

☐   ☐

32. Most people feel pretty good about the company.

☐   ☐

33. Management is pretty good at discussing its proposals with subordinates.

☐   ☐

34. Subordinates do not seem very involved in decisions related to their work.

☐   ☐

35. It's only by experience that you get to know the right people to go to.

☐   ☐

36. Bosses seem to keep changing their minds without consultation.

☐   ☐

37. Better results, it is felt, are obtained by involving everybody in the problems.

☐   ☐

38. The general direction of communication seems to be downward.

☐   ☐

39. Team work is a feature of everyday life.

☐   ☐

40. There seems to be a lot of informal and voluntary co-operation amongst most people in our organization.

☐   ☐

41. You're not paid to think in our company.

☐   ☐

Scoring key

Check back on your answer to each question and then refer to the score key which follows. You will need to set up two vertical columns on a separate piece of paper headed I and P. The numbers in the boxes on the score key should then be transferred to the appropriate column.

For example if you have agreed with statement 1 you score 2 under your I column. If you disagree you score 0. If you have agreed with statement 4 you score 1 under the I column and 1 under the P column. If you disagreed with question 4 you score 0.

When the totals under your I and P columns are added up they can be plotted as a single point (rather like plotting a map reference) on the quadrant provided.

		agree	*disagree*
1.	Everyone in the organization generally knows what contribution he makes to the whole.	2I	
2.	Management is not very approachable.		1P
3.	Loyalty to one's own department tends to come first.		1I
4.	Everyone is pleased when the company is successful.	1P 1I	
5.	People spend a lot of time blaming others for their own mistakes.		1I
6.	I generally know where to go when I want help.	1I	
7.	They tell us we are here to carry out instructions.		2P
8.	I am proud of the success of my company.	2P	
9.	Decisions always seem to come down from the top.		1P
10.	There seems to be quite a lot of friction and not much co-operation between departments.		2I

	agree	disagree
11. Management encourages superiors to discuss new proposals with their subordinates.	2P	
12. People normally consider the effect of their actions upon the whole organization.	1I	
13. The only way we learn of changes is by the grapevine.		1P 1I
14. It is not uncommon here to get conflicting orders and instructions.		2I
15. On the whole, people do not feel very free to speak their minds.		1P
16. People seem to prefer to get on with the job by themselves.		1I
17. One's job depends not so much on titles or activities but on what sort of position you can carve out for yourself.		1I
18. Normally staff are expected to accept orders without question.		2P
19. People in the organization only get together when there is a crisis.		1I
20. Managers place value on the opinions of subordinates.	2P	
21. In my job, I am rather unclear about what goes on in other functions.		2I
22. I don't think many people below senior management really understand the organization's objectives.		1P 1I
23. I often find it difficult to know who to approach for information.		1I

	agree	disagree
24. Managers seem more concerned about the narrow interest of their department rather than wider company objectives.		2I
25. Management is pretty intolerant of error and is not very good at listening to explanations.		1P
26. On the whole, communication in the company seems to be pretty full and free.	1P 1I	
27. In our company, subordinates are not afraid to say what they think.	1P 1I	
28. Wider participation in management is seen as a desirable objective by the organization.	2P	
29. All too often no one knows what his counterpart in another part of the organization is doing about things that affect them both.		2I
30. Managers tend to use their power to coerce subordinates.		1P
31. In our company, I think subordinates exercise quite a lot of influence on their bosses.	1P	
32. Most people feel pretty good about the company.	1P 1I	
33. Management is pretty good at discussing its proposals with subordinates.	2P	
34. Subordinates do not seem very involved in decisions related to their work.		1P
35. It's only by experience that you get to know the right people to go to.		1I
36. Bosses seem to keep changing their minds without consultation.		1P 1I
37. Better results, it is felt, are obtained by involving everybody in the problems.	1P	

	agree	disagree
38. The general direction of communication seems to be downward.		1P
39. Team work is a feature of everyday life.	2I	
40. There seems to be a lot of informal and voluntary co-operation amongst people in our organization.	1P 1I	
41. You're not paid to think in our company.		1P

Scoring Organization Profile

Check back on your answer to each question and then refer to the score key which follows. You will need to set up two verticle columns on a separate piece of paper headed I and P respectively. The numbers in the boxes on the score key should then be transferred to the appropriate column.

For example if you have agreed with question 1 you score 2 under your I column. If you disagree you score 0. If for question 4 you have agreed you score 1 under the I column and 1 under the P column. If you disagreed with question 4 you score 0.

When the totals under your I and P columns are added up they can be plotted as a single point (rather like plotting a map reference) on the quadrant provided.

Organizational profile

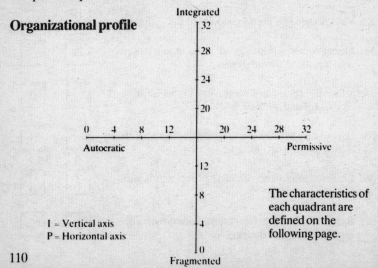

I = Vertical axis
P = Horizontal axis

The characteristics of each quadrant are defined on the following page.

Quadrant Characteristics

BUREAUCRATIC – Role Oriented	ORGANIC – Task Oriented
Role and status predominate	Overall task predominates
Communication up and down	Group consensus about decisions
Decision made by leader	Some shared influence
Answers sought/few ideas offered	Solutions sought jointly
Dependence on leader	High participation/high interaction
Moderate dependence on group	More ideas generated
Low interaction	High dependence on group
High leader satisfaction	Share satisfactions – lower for leader
AUTOCRATIC – Power Oriented	ANARCHIC – Person Oriented
Power/politics predominate	Individual personalities predominate
Answers demanded/rejected	No decision by group/sharing low
Anti-participation/divide & rule	Individual influence
Withholding of ideas	Low interaction/no participation
High integration against leader	Possessiveness about own ideas
Rejection of decision by group	Individual solutions
No dependence on group	Low dependence on group
Low satisfaction to members and leader	Individual satisfaction variable

THREE PHASES OF DEVELOPMENT

Linking together the ideas of Blake, Lievegoed, Greiner, and Sadler & Barry it is possible to see three quite distinct stages through which organizations move and I have chosen to refer to these as autocratic, bureaucratic, and democratic because the essential difference between them lies in the use of power and authority, and we can identify qualitative differences in this respect between these three phases. In my discussion of the three phases from now on I shall refer to them as Phase 1 (Autocratic), Phase 2 (Bureaucratic) and Phase 3 (Democratic).

You may find it helpful, as we look in more detail at the characteristics or organizations in each phase, to try and identify organizations you know – or departments within them – and see where they fit in the model. With a little practice it is not too difficult. Don't be surprised, though, if you occasionally find an organization which appears to be in all three stages at once. This just helps us to remember that the world can't be sorted into three boxes so easily. It has also been referred to as Sods Law!

Phase 1: The autocratic phase.

The essential characteristics of Phase 1 in the development of the organization is the role played by the pioneer, the founder, the man who creates the organization. He is the source of strength, the driving force, usually in the direction of creating a product and a market.

The autocratic phase itself goes through stages in development. At the beginning, survival is the main problem, for the failure rate is high. One only has to look at recent government figures on failed new businesses to see that. Once survival is ensured, rapid growth is likely because of the intrinsic advantages of the auto-cratic pioneer organization, such as quick decision-making, clear leadership, personal control, flexibility, good customer service, low overheads, and staff involvement.

This growth may go on for many years although it is unusual for it to last less than ten or fifteen years. There are forces at work inevitably causing the growth rate to slow down. The rot may begin many years before it becomes apparent and obvious. It may be brought about by increasing competition, changing technology and social conditions, obsolescence of product design or machinery, but the major cause lies in the pioneer and his or her management style. It is natural, perhaps inevitable, that pioneers should keep the decision-making power and authority in their own hands. The business grows round them in a 'maypole' structure and to begin with they may have to fill the major management functions themselves, personally controlling production, sales, finance and staff. They know everybody and every facet of their business. They exercise 'eyeball control'. They run a very tight ship and take a pride in doing so.

There comes a stage, however, when the intrinsic defects in this autocratic management can begin to show through. As the pioneer grows older and the organization grows bigger, the burden becomes too heavy for him or her to shoulder alone. But there is no one to delegate to, because no management structure has been built up, and no one has been encouraged to take decisions. The pioneer may introduce managers from outside, but it is rare that he or she will delegate authority effectively, until it is taken out of their hands (e.g. Henry Ford when he was 83, Helena Rubenstein when she was 93).

There comes a stage when the organization goes into a stage of very rapid decline, entering what Lievegoed calls 'the crisis of the first phase' and Greiner 'the crisis of autonomy'.

This process is shown very clearly in the rise and fall of Henry Ford I, summarized below, a story with many parallels.

The rise and fall of Henry Ford (the history of a pioneer)

1863	Born at Dearborn, Michigan.
1903	Ford Company established with capital of $28,000 and eleven partners. 1,708 cars produced that year.
1913	200,000 cars. (All partners had been bought out.)
1914	Ford doubles wages from $2.50 to $5.00. He is hailed as a most progressive employer, even by the Russian Bolsheviks.
1915	Half a million cars.
1923	Two million cars.
1923/25	Two-thirds of car market in USA is Ford's. Model T still the only model.
1927	Need to retool for new Model A Ford to meet General Motors competition. 60,000 workers laid off.
1928	*New York Times* calls Ford 'an industrial fascist', the 'Mussolini of Detroit'.

1936	The Ford Company has a force of over 3,000 company police, headed by policeman Bennet (who becomes Henry's righthand man). Ford Foundation established (Ford family controls 40 per cent of votes).
1941	Ford forced to allow entry of unions into his plants.
1943	Death of his son Edsel.
1946	Ford Company losing $10 million per month. The company starts legal proceedings to displace old Henry, now 83 years old (pioneers do not give up easily).
1948	Henry Ford II brings in Breech from General Motors to help build up an organization structure.

(Based on *Working for Ford* by H. Beynon.)

Stages within the autocratic phase

It is possible to show the ups and downs in Phase 1 diagramatically.

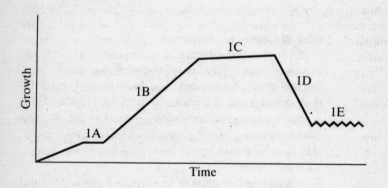

Key   1A Survival phase
      1B Rapid growth
      1C Levelling off
      1D Decline
      1E Crisis

Obviously, there will be individual differences in organizations and the time element may vary considerably. The organization described in the vision-building section reached its Phase 1 crisis in sixteen years. The crucial factor is the quality of management – especially the degree of awareness and the skill in recognizing and reacting to the signals of crisis. In terms of resistance I suggest that the most difficult time to implement significant changes will be in stages 1C, 1D and the early part of 1E because the system is putting most of its energies into defensive activity.

The importance of Phase 1

It is well known how animal groups develop an order of dominance, or 'pecking' order, under a single leader. This order is accepted by the group and remains stable as long as the leadership can retain control and fend off challenges to his leadership. It is not surprising, therefore, that autocracy, in one form or another, has been the main organizational form in human groups as well, and was the natural form adopted by the modern organization. Other forms of organization, such as bureaucracy and democracy, are not easily evolved or readily accepted, and are continually threatened by a reversion to autocracy, particularly in times of crisis.

Autocratic management lives on in most organizations long after new forms have been developed, as does the impact of the founder of the organization. The pioneer's values, attitudes, and mode of operating leave an impact which accounts largely for the corporate personality or culture which each organization develops, as seen for example in the Ford Motor Company, IBM, Racal, Marks & Spencer.

Much of the folklore and practice of management originates from this pioneer phase, for example the hard-nosed approach, profit maximization, tight control, accountability, reluctance to delegate, secretiveness, individualism, management by authority, and the deification of the strong manager. The pioneer develops a charisma seldom found amongst later managers. This is well deserved, as the pioneer creates something where nothing existed before. The greatest folklore is, of course, the rate of growth and success.

115

It is well to remember that though in its classic form pioneer autocratic management is associated with the Victorian and Edwardian eras, most small businesses still tend to be run in this way, and that new pioneers are constantly emerging and posing a threat to the larger and older establishments, because of their mobility, flexibility and decision-making advantages. Smaller computer companies such as Apple did exactly that to IBM in the personal computer market.

The crisis of Phase 1

Lievegoed writes: 'Growth continues within a certain structure until a limit is reached; beyond this limit the existing structure or model can no longer impose order on mass, the consequence is either disintegration or a step up to a higher level of order.'

Growth in size, complexity, and age bring Phase 1 in an organization to an end. Something has to be done to prevent disintegration. New management is required which will develop new structure and approaches to make good what was missing or inadequately developed in Phase 1, namely management and organization structure, systems and procedures, distribution of authority, better planning and different forms of control.

It is at this stage that the pioneer has to make critical choices about his own growth and that of the organization. Some pioneers want to stay pioneers and resist the drift into a larger, more bureaucratic phase of development. However, if the business is successful it will inevitably happen and the choice becomes a personal one for the pioneer. Does he become head of a large bureaucratic system or does he go and 'pioneer' somewhere else? The crisis here is both organizational and personal.

Phase 2: The bureaucratic phase

The most distinctive feature of an organization in this phase is the way it is structured. Here everything is spelled out. Every job has its description. Indeed, in full bloom, the bureaucratic phase organization is, quite literally, a well-organized machine.

We can sum up the essence of bureaucratic management as:

1. Division of work in an orderly and stable fashion.
2. Systematization of rules and procedures.
3. Establishment of a hierarchy in which lower ranks are governed by higher.
4. Distribution of authority through a number of levels in a systematic manner.
5. Promotion on the basis of qualifications and experience.
6. Rules and procedures override the requirements of the situation.

The mechanistic quality of the bureaucratic phase is both its strength and weakness, and the driving force for a more flexible system in the next phase. Bureaucratic models and ethics have, however, been of great value to organizations. It is fashionable to dismiss bureaucracy as cumbersome, rigid and rather *passé*, but I find in many situations a good dose of systematic procedures and order is what is needed in an organization. There have been many occasions when, if I had followed my own values, inclinations and intuition, I would have recommended to an organization management styles and systems more appropriate to Phase 3. This would have matched my own preferences. It is at times like this that developmental frameworks are so helpful. What the organization in fact needed was some order and structure to control its growth. So what are the major benefits of bureaucracy?

— It provides the organization structure for the management of large-scale enterprises.

— It makes possible the delegation and co-ordination of power and authority.

— It establishes management on a systematic, as opposed to haphazard, basis.

— It produces major advances in efficiency.

— It improves the working conditions of labour and the human relations involved.

117

— It makes possible tremendous advances in technology through research and development.

— It produces a systematic theory of management where little or nothing existed before.

Its defects, however, are increasingly apparent:

— The system overrides the requirements of the situation.

— Initiative may be smothered.

— The impersonal nature of the system undermines motivation.

— Decision-making is slow.

— The system is rigid and changes slowly.

— It is not well suited to a turbulent and rapidly changing environment.

— The emphasis is on precedent rather than the future. Old solutions are applied to new problems.

— Power, status and privileges are entrenched.

Bureaucracy is short-lived compared to the autocratic pioneer phase of organizations. It is a relatively modern invention developed to cope with rapid growth in size and complexity. There are nevertheless many examples. The Civil Service must be the classic one. Bureaucracy still has value but with the rate of change and degree of turbulence we live in nowadays the issue is usually how an organization can benefit from the order and structure of Phase 2 without being strangled by it. I am personally convinced that Lievegoed was right in maintaining that one cannot simply skip over Phase 2. Development is sequential and movement towards Phase 3 must involve the establishment of a sound base in Phase 2.

For example, it is no use having a highly competent, forward looking, participative management team in place without a firm infrastructure of policies and procedures to bring about co-ordination and progress. People need to be clear about their responsibilities, what is expected of them and the parameters within which they can work. These are all 'bureaucratic' processes.

Stages within the autocratic and bureaucratic phases

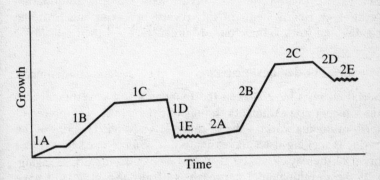

Key

Phase 1	Autocracy	Phase 2	Bureaucracy
1A	Survival phase	2A	Survival phase
1B	Rapid growth	2B	Rapid growth
1C	Levelling off	2C	Levelling off
1D	Decline	2D	Decline
1E	Crisis	2E	Crisis

As early as 1955, Peter Drucker wrote: 'At some unmarked point during the last twenty years we imperceptibly moved out of the modern age and into a new, as yet nameless, era. The old view of the world, the old tasks and the old centre, calling themselves modern and up to date only a few years ago, just make no sense any more. We have no theories, no concepts, no slogans – no real knowledge – about the new reality.'

It is possible that the explosion of the atomic bomb may have sparked off Drucker's perceptive statement about the new reality. It was change of a qualitative nature with vast implications. Since then we have seen the growth of atomic power, space travel, supersonic flight, the rise of information technology, the spread of television, laser and fibre optics, and numerous other developments in technology of a radical kind.

Whilst Phase 2 is likely to become less relevant to today's and tomorrow's fast-moving business environment, we still need to build on its strengths as a foundation for moving forward into the much more exciting, but less predictable, Phase 3. Information technology clearly helps in this regard by taking much of the rigidity and work volume out of bureaucracy – if used sensibly.

Phase 3: The democratic phase

Social changes have shaken the foundations of government and the existing establishments throughout the world. The power of the 'developing world' – the so-called less advanced nations of the earth, is making itself increasingly felt. Global markets are the order of the day.

If the developmental approach is of any use, it should have predictive value in helping us to understand what is happening and what is ahead. Let us see what Phase 3 organizations might have to cope with before we explore how they look.

1. *Magnitude*
   Population growth will dwarf any conceptions we have had in the past of size of organizations.

2. *Quality*
   Populations will not only be larger, but of a different quality in terms of education, ability and aspirations.

3. *Complexity*
   Quantitative and qualitative changes will result in new levels of complexity, requiring new approaches and new thinking.

4. *Urgency*
   Because of the size and speed of operations, pressures will build up rapidly, so that problems will have to be solved speedily.

5. *Acceptability*

Solutions will have to be acceptable to more educated and more sophisticated populations.

6. *Humanity*

Solutions will have to be humane, providing for the needs of all levels of the population, not only those of the privileged sections.

7. *Elegance*

'Elegant' solutions, that is, solutions with the highest all-round excellence, will be favoured and these will often be of a temporary nature in view of the speed of change.

8. *Collaboration*

Atomic power accentuates the need for collaboration internationally; and nationally no adequate solutions can be found without collaboration between different interest groups. Solutions must be of a win-win rather than a win-lose nature.

9. *Service*

Organizations in which service rather than profit is the criterion will play an increasingly dominant role in this 'post-industrial' society.

These are the main issues which will already be facing many of you as you try to move your organization towards Phase 3.

The democratic phase is difficult to describe because we have relatively little experience of it yet, and many of us are struggling to make emerging Phase 3 organizations work. The components are already familiar to us, such as teamwork, clear corporate goals, individual spontaneity, open communication, commitment, flexibility, adaptable structures, involvement, and so on. I don't know yet of many organizations well established enough in Phase 3 to provide us with a good model of the totality, but there are some that are moving very rapidly and successfully in this direction – the Burton Group to name but one.

What we can do is look at what we know to be the component characteristics of Phase 3 organizations.

Summary of democratic phase characteristics organization structure

— Clover-leaf organization – with the executive team at the centre of a communication system.
— Interlocking groups.
— Temporary task teams and project groups.

Management emphasis

— Innovation and development.
— Goal orientation.
— Problem-solving.
— High-performance goals.
— Team achievement.

Management style

— Teamwork with individual responsibilities and confrontation of difficulties.
— Participative.
— Supportive.
— Low Control.

Controls

— Task achievements – individual and team.
— Mutual goal-setting.
— High standards.
— Learning from mistakes.

In more operational terms we can itemize the major features of the democratic phase as follows:

1. Setting of both short- and long-term goals and objectives is the basis of the management system.

2. Participation in this process by different levels of management is vital.

3. Though individual contribution is encouraged, it is as a member of a team. Teamwork is considered of major importance.

4. Interpersonal relationships are supportive rather than competitive, and aim towards making each person feel that his or her contribution is worthwhile.

5. Authority is based on competence and collaboration rather than power or threat.

6. The distance between top and bottom levels of management is lessened by a wider distribution of decision-making powers.

7. This is made possible by clearer definition of policies, within which the individual has freedom of operation.

8. Participation and involvement exist in order to get the best out of each individual rather than simply to minimize resistance and buy compliance.

9. Staff motivation is prompted by allowing individuals greater control over their work, within the limits of policies and objectives.

10. Achieving objectives supercedes obeying instructions.

11. Confidence and trust are built by open communications and frank discussion of difficulties.

12. Training and development of staff are considered of prime importance and are continuously encouraged.

13. Rewards are related to achievement of objectives. These are more group oriented and less of a piecework incentive nature.

14. Distinctions between hourly and monthly paid staff are diminished. There is a general move towards salaried staff conditions for all.

15. The organization is viewed as an open system in which balanced treatment must be ensured to all sub-groups, shareholders, employees, customers and suppliers.

16. The emphasis shifts from management development to organization development, that is, the development of the organization as a whole rather than the training of managers in isolation.

17. Maximum output (volume or quality) is aimed at by removing stoppages caused by departmental and individual conflict and parochial interests.

18. The organization is seen as part of the community and its obligations to the community are accepted.

19. Adaptability and flexibility of operation are of paramount importance, and these are achieved by frequent *ad hoc* assessments of the situation as opposed to the dictates of a system.

20. Temporary task systems will flourish – some of a pioneering nature.

These twenty characteristics provide a useful checklist against which to assess your own organization. Some of them you will undoubtedly recognize as being in place and others as more hopeful than actual. This is my vision of a Phase 3 organization and there is increasing evidence that as an ideal to work towards it is both difficult and necessary. The list is in no way intended to be complete but it highlights the enormous task facing you as managers in moving the organization towards Phase 3.

THE PRINCIPLES OF DEVELOPMENT

In conclusion, we can sum up some of the general principles to be drawn from the developmental approach. The following could be thought of as the ten commandments of organization development. I have found them extremely useful, especially when the behaviour of managers seems to be out of phase with the stage of development and life looks very messy and confusing.

1. Organizations are 'open systems'.

2. They evolve through recognizable phases which are an expression of internal growth factors and environmental pressures.

3. The age, size and history of an organization are important determinants of organization structure and management systems.

4. The development from one phase to another involves qualitative changes accompanied by periods of crisis or turbulence.

5. In this process it is necessary to distinguish between growth, i.e. increase in size, and development, i.e. change in structure and nature.

6. Development is not necessarily continuous or linear.

7. Each phase is both a consequence of the previous phase and a cause of the next.

8. Remnants of earlier phases linger on in the next and cause tensions.

9. Solutions which are adequate in one phase may not be adequate in the next.

10. In order to take corrective action and assess what lies ahead it is important to determine the stage in development reached by the organization.

The attraction of the developmental approach is that it does not exclude other approaches, but provides a frame of reference within which they can be located or assessed. It is a macro rather than micro approach and, most important, it does seem to relate to managers' reality.

APPLYING THE DEVELOPMENTAL APPROACH

Every organization needs to analyse what stage it has reached in its own developmental history in order to see the way ahead. At the same time, every organization is caught up in larger social or technological developments on a national and international scale, over which the individual organization has no control. If it remains stationary or goes against the mainstream it does so at considerable risk. As a first step in thinking about organizational survival and development, appropriate management actions must be identified, based on the needs of the evolving organization rather than the whims or values of individual managers.

Whilst one can generalize about development stages at the level of the total system, and about appropriate change strategies, it should not be forgotten that within an organization there will be sub-systems which are at different phases of their own development. They may well need to be treated in a somewhat different way. However, the main concern from the perspective of developing relevant strategies for change is to focus on the boundaries of the sub-systems. They will need to be carefully managed if they are to remain integrated and connected to the overall shift of direction. In some cases, for example, certain departments will already be moving into the next phase of development – or may already have arrived there. A typical example of this phenomenon is the systems department of a large bureaucratic company where the effectiveness of the systems group in influencing the mainstream of the business depends almost entirely on how well the systems manager manages his boundary with the rest of the organization. If this is done well the rest of the organization is able to learn from it and can be helped forward. In my own consulting experience the boundaries, unfortunately, are more often a battleground of misunderstanding and frustration because the behaviour processes are poorly understood and not managed.

The most dramatic example of misfit I have experienced was in a mail order company which was a family concern and had been successful for many years. It was in its crisis of the first phase. The business had outgrown the family entrepreneurs and it was struggling to devolve some managerial authority to professional managerial staff.

I was invited in by the training and personnel director who was totally committed to managerial concepts and values consistent with a Phase 3, democratic, organization. It gradually became clear that what the organization was demanding in the way of developmental activities and training was focused almost exclusively on preparing managers for Phase 3 – flexibility, temporary task team management, participation, negotiated goals and objectives. This was in accord with the personnel director's values, and with my own. But was it relevant to the organization's stage of development? No.

One thing which bugged the growth and effective management of the company at this time was the lack of systems and procedures to control and administer purchasing, stock control, distribution and associated records for marketing purposes – all the signs that some good healthy bureaucracy was needed. The trick was not to overdo it.

We did develop some temporary teams but focused them specifically on developing the fundamental bureaucratic systems needed to move the company away from its top management-dominated decision-making processes towards a delegated and regularized set of systems.

Without the concept of phases of development and involvement, participation and team development activities requested by the personnel department could have flowered and withered in a short time due to having no firm Phase 2 base on which to grow.

There are also some interesting examples which I have recently encountered travelling in India. In talking to a number of Indian businessmen and managers it seems clear that many Indian organizations are beginning to experience signs of crisis. But if we refer to the model – which crisis? In order to be sure we need to look at the political and economic environment. In most cases the multinationals have sold out and their place has been taken by Indian entrepreneurs building large, successful trading houses and conglomerates. These companies, of which BIRLA and TATA, for example, are typical, are major success stories and have followed the classic developmental route. They are very much pioneering organizations, still driven by their larger than life charismatic entrepreneurs, but they are too large to continue for long in this way and are fast approaching the crisis of Phase 1.

The companies who are at crisis are the long-standing colonial ones which still run on strongly authoritarian, bureaucratic lines, where the authority lies firmly in the role rather than in the individual's competence. This certainly sounds like a recipe for major crisis, especially in the case of certain industries like banking which is about to experience computerization on a massive scale, and is keenly recruiting the best MBA graduates it can get. There is likely to be an extended period of considerable turbulence in these organizations, while the diverse interests of the various parties (powerful senior managers and systems specialists, and young, ambitious MBAs whose values and organizational concepts are – I believe – much more akin to Phase 3 organizations) are somehow reconciled.

WHERE ARE WE NOW? A PROCESS VIEW

The developmental approach to diagnosis focuses on a framework for identifying the position of the organization on its journey. The process view, which we will now move on to, takes us underneath the surface to explore in more detail the subtleties of behaviour and emotional processes that accompany the various stages of development and crisis.

The organization iceberg

The analogy of the iceberg is relevant because most of an iceberg's bulk is below the surface, just as most of the things one bumps into whilst trying to change something in an organization are also concealed under the surface, residing in what is often called the informal organization and what I call the submerged organization.

If we look at the visible part of the iceberg we see all the aspects of the organization with which we are familiar and which are usually *managed* quite effectively by managers:

— Technology
— Formal roles and job titles
— Organization structure
— Job description
— Policies and objectives
— Procedures
— Formal communication structures
— Reporting relationships
— Products and services

These aspects of the organization are consciously managed and, generally, rewards are distributed on the basis of how well they are seen to be managed. So effort expended on these aspects is often considerable, since they are precisely the areas where results bring rewards.

These are the aspects of the organization we understand because they are *rational* and *logical*. They are also the ones which are constantly subject to changes of one sort or another. Whether the organization goes through any real or lasting change, however, depends entirely upon how much energy is injected into influencing the submerged, murky, and often uncharted depths of the iceberg below the surface. Some of the factors to be found in this submerged organization are:

— Norms
— Beliefs and values
— Personal aspirations and goals
— Management style and values
— Power networks
— Informal relationships
— Attitudes
— Loyalties
— Motivations and commitments
— Perceived rewards

Managing content and process – the 'what' and the 'how'

Scenario 1

The personnel director has just spent weeks sifting through the 'potential' files to find a successor to a departmental manager. It is a key appointment and many bright stars have been considered. After considerable thought and senior management time the post is offered to David Crockett. He says 'no thank you'. The personnel director goes spare. What went wrong?

Scenario 2

A large company in the insurance sector has a head office in London and is increasingly moving its staff to its new administrative centre in the West Country. It announces one Friday that the whole of its underwriting department will be moving from London to the West Country over the next few months. In an unprecedented move, the whole underwriting department agrees to send a deputation to management telling them that they refuse to move. What went wrong?

In the two scenarios mentioned, there may be nothing wrong with *what* was actually decided. The decisions may well have been correct. What got in the way was the *process* involved in *how* the decisions were arrived at. Had the personnel director involved potential candidates even to the extent of asking them whether they wanted to be considered he may have saved a lot of valuable time and eventual frustration. Likewise, in the second case some thought about individual needs and aspirations and about how the incumbents mights be influenced to support the plan at an earlier stage would have saved considerable embarrassment all round.

Simple examples, but with the same clear message. Easy in hindsight – but we don't usually do it.

We are good at managing *content*, the '*what*', but poor at managing *process*, the '*how*'. Not enough time is allowed to *reflect* on the way in which the change might be brought about.

As managers we focus heavily on *content* as a result of our technical training and inclination towards a rational view of the world, which is so much part of our cultural heritage in the West. The submerged parts of the iceberg, or *organizational processes*, are mostly non-linear, non-rational and often confusing social and political processes; dealing with them requires intuitive skills and awareness rather than sharp, logical analysis.

The organizational diagram that follows shows a flow from input to output on the task level which is very often impeded by the underlying stream of behaviour, procedures and feelings (as indicated by the broken line) that pop out and block progress. This interruption has little to do with the rationale of the task being undertaken but has everything to do with the politics and relationships surrounding the task. For example, if a department is increasing its organizational power base through the achievement of a particular key project, it can be in the interests of departments or individuals who currently hold the power to block progress of that project. You only have to watch and listen to the antics at regular meetings to see what I mean. Next time you attend a meeting jot down the percentage of time given to *task* items on the agenda and the amount given to 'political' and 'personal' agendas. You will see what I mean. For a good grounding in understanding political and behavioural processes in organizations as well as interpersonal processes one could do a lot worse than watch a few episodes of *Dallas* or *Dynasty*.

The skilful manager of change, however, is good at spotting the signals and will sense that process issues are 'bubbling' and allocate time and energy to managing them, so that the disruption they cause is minimal.

Organizational Process

Awareness of process is not, in itself, sufficient. It has to be consciously managed. This is easier said than done because most organizations reward their managers for managing tasks not processes. How many objectives have you agreed to or had set for you this year which allude to the *way you manage* staff appraisals, meetings, delegation, interdepartmental boundaries, etc? Probably not many. Objectives are set to achieve task results. In the

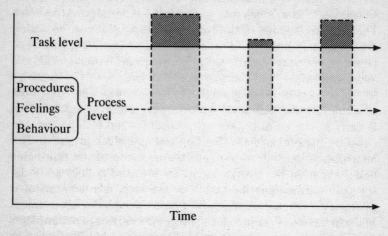

Time

Key

Process issues 'break' the surface and interrupt work on task

Process issues are 'bubbling' under the surface

Effective task working

Effective process

management of change, however, this is a recipe for failure. *The process must be managed consciously.* Strategies, tactics and objectives need to be agreed in relation to *how* change will be brought about as well as *what* will be done.

I have recently come across an example of this in an international organization in India. The organization is about to enter a period of major upheaval due to computerization of large parts of its manual operation. This will involve virtually all the local and expatriate staff. The technical planning (the *content*) has been carefully done and a model system is being set up in the training centre for every staff member to become familiar, in safe surroundings, with the new systems of working. There is a good recognition that since the last major technology change was the switch from red and black ink to ballpoint pens in 1960, the switch to computers will be traumatic! However, there is also the issue of the process by which these changes will be communicated and discussed. The content planning and content training has been well thought out, but so far the *process* planning is nonexistent. It is known, for example, that the style and management culture of the organization is autocratic and paternalistic. Communications is relatively closed and downwards only. The general manager recognizes that staff will have to be communicated with consistently during the changes if he is to avoid problems from the militant unions. In his own words, 'We've got to explain to the staff what, why and how we're going to do it.'

He is absolutely correct, but at the moment there is no more than a vain hope that somehow this will happen. It is not seen as legitimate to expend managerial energy and resources on developing the infrastructures needed (such as consultation procedures, briefing groups, discussion, training for supervisors, etc.) to enable this communication process to take place. But unless this process is managed, the change is likely to be difficult, long drawn out and more expensive than it otherwise need be. The cost to the organization in the end will be much greater than the cost of managing the process now.

As we have seen, understanding organizational growth and development is a key ingredient in the manager's understanding of how to handle changes. The processes to be found submerged below the surface of the iceberg during the various stages of development are very different and there is often a tendency to make assumptions based on past experience which are well out of date and out of place with current reality. A vivid example is often that of an organization which has been taken over, such as the Seat of the Pants Insurance Company.

The Seat of the Pants Insurance Company: A case study

The Seat of the Pants Insurance Company was fifteen years old, had a rapid growth record in size of premium growth, profitability and numbers of staff. It was characterized by the founder's energy, exuberance, high-risk style of business and considerable success. There were few rules, a lot of informality, always frenetic activity and regular blunders which were accepted and put right. Everyone felt involved, worked hard, complained constantly about the pressure – and loved every minute of it.

Then Seat of the Pants was absorbed into the Failsafe Corporation – a large financial services company with a long success record over ninety years, having developed from a Penny Bank.

Seat of the Pants had the usual problems of restructuring, instituting procedures and harmonizing policies, salaries, pensions and so on, and after a year or two looked remarkably like Failsafe – on paper.

All the *task* level indicators suggested a continued growth and profitability pattern but a look at the *process* level – how people were actually behaving – showed a very different story. For example – enormous energy was now expended on managing the political boundaries between Failsafe and Seat of the Pants. So much so that energy left for enthusiastic risk-taking and working long hours was minimal. And there was a subtle change in the type of complaining people did – it became more plaintive and hopeless.

Failsafe began to apply its parental, middle-aged assumptions to jack up the performance of its new acquisition, and got a typical adolescent response rather than an adult one. A mixture of sullen, rebellious and wholly emotional behaviour.

Management of the boundary between these two systems would have been considerably easier given a sensitive understanding of the differences in their stages of maturity and development and some attempt to manage the different behaviour processes involved. As it is I suspect a great deal of productive energy will continue to be wasted fighting across the borders for some time to come. Both systems could be losers, at least in the short term.

Dealing with content and process in parallel

Our whole culture and way of thinking is built on dealing with series of events in sequential order. We are trained at schools and universities to think rationally, logically and *sequentially*. For example 'planning comes before implementing' – *wrong*.

In managing change effectively, Eastern cultures have one great advantage, which is the ability to view life as a continuous cyclic process rather than a series of sequential and discrete events. This makes it much easier for them to consider planning, designing and implementing changes as a continuous, integrated and *parallel* set of processes. The ability to understand and really internalize this concept is absolutely critical to the success of change over the longer term – unless of course one is in the fortunate position of having and maintaining absolute power! It is my experience that whilst this concept of parallel implementation is not difficult to understand as an intellectual concept, it is extraordinarily difficult for managers to actually 'behave' it in practice. Not only is time pressure against it, but our Western culture militates against it too. It is nevertheless an absolute key to effective management of evolutionary change.

In my teaching and consultancy roles I work with managers on issues of formulation and implementation of strategic change. There is one exercise which I regularly use in this context which is essentially very straightforward but which consistently illustrates the problem managers have in bringing into their actual behaviour the concept of managing process.

First of all we talk about the concept of parallel implementation and managing process. There is general agreement that consideration must be given to *how* implementation will take place, what pitfalls or resistances might need to be addressed and planned for, *at the same time as* planning is done on *what* needs to change. So far so good.

We then work in two groups – a group of planners and a group of implementers. The planners have to work out how to instruct the implementing team to carry out a fairly complex assembly task. The planners must not do any of the assembly, they must simply draw up a plan for instructing the implementers to do it.

The implementers are told to wait in another room and organize themselves as best they can within the uncertainty that exists. They are also asked to record their feelings and attitudes toward the planning team. Neither group has any constraints on contact with the other team. I am sure you can predict the outcome, and it would never happen to you – would it?

In almost every case the two groups don't meet within the time allotted for the exercise. If they do, it is almost always at the instigation of the implementers who then receive short shrift from the busy planners who are totally engrossed in their 'task'.

Once again a powerful reminder that *task-content* is very seductive and *process* has been ignored. When the planners deliver the results of their technical hard work to the implementing group they find behaviour ranging from disinterest to obstruction and feelings ranging from anger to 'demob happy'. Some implementing groups go on strike and refuse to 'play'. There are many organizational parallels for this.

The message is painfully clear. Early attention by planners to the management of their sub-system boundary will minimize a great deal of aggravation and resistance.

Senior management very often beaver away on a difficult long-term plan without discussing it with other managers 'because we don't have anything final or sensible to say yet'. By this stage it may already be too late. If they are lucky and have willing, compliant middle managers they will get away with it – but their credit in the good will account will be greatly diminished.

Tell your middle managers something – even if it's an explanation of the difficulties you're having. They might even have an idea or two!

Open system thinking can help in the sense that if, as a planner, one sees the 'system' as including planners and implementers, it helps to raise the question, 'How do we manage the relationship?' Even more importantly, it raises the question, 'What is the *objective* of this *total system*?'

A closed system view

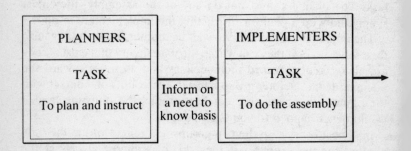

136

An open system view

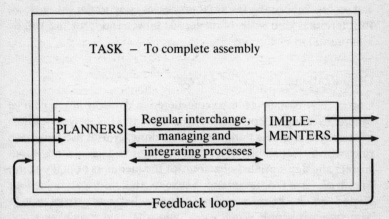

There are three good reasons why working on WHAT and HOW in parallel is important: *obtaining commitment* early on; *sustaining motivation* as the project progresses; and *achieving task results*.

As my experience with this exercise and in organizations repeatedly demonstrates, achieving task results is the one area which organizational reward systems reinforce and encourage; the other two get done only if a manager happens to value that aspect of managing.

For effective change management these three components have to be given equal weight. Equal attention to *what* and *how* is the way to achieve this.

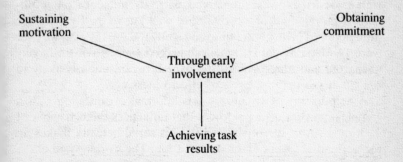

The importance of recognizing, and managing, these factors cannot be over-emphasized. They are the very things that get up and bite you if you try to make changes by simply tinkering with the formal system and ignore the informal processes lying under the surface. It is here that your skills of diagnosis, power and influence will be at a premium.

Organizational and group norms

One of the first aspects to be considered in deciding *how* a change should be brought about is the nature of norms in the system which exist concerning how things should be done. Norms are unwritten rules which exist in all social systems and provide guidelines about correct and appropriate behaviour for the members of that system. The trick is to differentiate between the informal behaviour carried on in the name of tradition, habit and expectation – namely, what people *actually do* – and what senior managers, job descriptions and chairmen's statements to shareholders *tell you* they do. There is usually a world of difference between the two and the skilful manager will be able to spot the difference quickly. This is not quite as easy as it sounds on paper, especially if you are living inside the system you are trying to understand. Perception, once again, plays a part and the filters of what you *expect* to see can easily distort what is actually happening. However, the key here is to watch actual behaviour; this gives many clues to norm patterns.

Dozens of studies have documented the effect on the organization of its informal/submerged part. Its influence on profitability, morale and productivity are well known and yet we are little better at giving it the time and study it deserves than we ever were. As long as the informal/submerged aspects remain largely uncharted and unrecognized the overall organization is likely to remain at sub-optimal levels of effectiveness.

A helpful way of visualizing this informal organization is as a complex network of social forces that influences the behaviour of each member of the organization. This social network makes up the normative system of the organization. The working unit of the normative system is the norm – simply defined as *behaviour that is anticipated and expected by the group of its members*. Norms operate everywhere – in families, work groups, gangs, organizations, clubs. They represent the tissue that joins social fabric together, and without them life would be very difficult and disoriented.

Organizations can be viewed, like societies, as highly complex cultures with their own normative structures. In fact the cultures frequently become the rationale for the actual functioning of the organization. Creative or innovative managers will soon learn, in some companies, that to avoid criticism it is better to keep their opinions to themselves and play it safe. In others the name of the game is to 'appear' to be constantly busy and never have time to stop and talk. Results may be less important than being seen to be busy and always late leaving the office. Some companies promote helpful, compliant people into managerial roles for many different reasons, not the least of which is that they are easier to control from the top, thus preserving the autocratic Phase 1 ethos. The important common thread here is that those reasons have little or nothing to do with the rational one of effective running of the business – they have to do with staying within normative patterns, and the problem is that these behavioural norms are often at odds with corporate or departmental objectives.

Norms are 'powerful medicine'

Some years ago I worked in a large petro-chemical company which had – and still has – a worldwide reputation as a progressive employer, especially in its personnel policies. There had been a policy in operation for several years, reinforced by a staff appraisal scheme, that managers would be promoted on the basis of two key criteria – technical competence in their area of expertise, and leadership and organizational ability. This was the top of the iceberg speaking – and it was passionately believed and promulgated regularly by most top managers and personnel staff. Underneath the water, however, managers received a different message which they deduced from their actual experience (rather than what was said). What actually happened was that each time a senior management appointment was made it was seen that the recipient was the best technical person available but rarely a competent leader or organizational manager. So what was said, and reinforced by training and procedures, differed from line experience. This only began to be changed when a conscious, and publicized, attempt was made to break the mould by appointing a competent engineer into the technical director's job and letting it be known that as well as being the best technical man available he was an excellent personnel and organizational manager. Some indication of how strong norms are can be gained from the fact that the reaction was initially one of disbelief, followed by 'oh well, it's just a flash in the pan'. Gradually it was accepted that 'maybe' it was the beginning of change.

Norms are often developed with little conscious awareness by the very people and organizations whose lives they are moulding. So a work group or organization may have a norm of mediocrity or 'don't rock the boat', without the people inside that system ever considering consciously whether they prefer mediocrity to a search for excellent performance. Again, it's rather like the goldfish syndrome – easy to see the water from the outside but unaware that you are in it until someone changes or disturbs it. It is not surprising that changes that upset or threaten norms create such violent reactions and often have to be initiated from outside. New employees joining the work group are rapidly enmeshed in the web of existing structures and are rewarded by their peers and managers for conforming to existing patterns. An individual joining the work group who shows dissatisfaction with the routine will be encouraged to see the error of his ways and will be brought into line – he may in extreme cases be encouraged to leave.

I have, on occasions, been asked to do some counselling in organizations and found that what was actually wanted was someone to 're-educate' certain senior people who needed to be brought into line with the way things were done in the company. In one company it was openly stated that this was a last chance before the final process of 'counselling out', as they quaintly described their dismissal (perish the word) procedure, was activated.

These unwritten rules tend to have greater influence on organizational effectiveness than perhaps any other single factor. When they are negative and destructive, whatever the company does will be less effective than it might otherwise have been. On the other hand, when they are positive they are an enormous asset to decision-making, to standards of individual, group and corporate performance, to training, development, innovation, and to management effectiveness.

Norms are a hindrance to change

A key point for managers involved in change is that those norms which are strongly positive today may be a millstone to progress in a different phase of organization development. For example, if we take the financial services sector, norms of steadiness, loyalty, order and thrift have been of enormous strength in the long-term success of banks and building societies but they are already proving to be great threats to risk-taking, radical innovation and survival in an increasingly turbulent world where Phase 3 values are more relevant. On the other hand, there are at the moment a number of examples of organizations, currently very successful, where all the norms of the pioneering Phase 1 – rapid growth, high return on investment, entrepreneurial risk-taking and fast movement – have operated successfully over ten or fifteen years. These norms are very deeply rooted and are perpetuated through recruitment and promotion. As the companies grow into the next stage of development, the bureaucratic phase, norms will be needed concerning systematization, co-ordination and stability that do not yet exist. It is at these points in a company's development, when transition points and crises become very evident, that inappropriate norms can be disastrous.

Research by Allen & Pilnick identified ten general clusters of norms – both positive and negative – which seemed to have most impact on the effective performance of organizations. Companies and departments with positive norms in those clusters tended to be more successful in their achievement of organization objectives. I have found these clusters can provide a useful diagnostic tool for the analysis of organizations in change, and will therefore take some time to elaborate on them.

The ten norm clusters were as follows:

1. Organizational and personal pride
2. Performance/excellence
3. Teamwork/communication

4. Leadership/supervision
5. Profitability and cost effectiveness
6. Colleague relationships
7. Customer and consumer relations
8. Honesty and security
9. Training and development
10. Innovation and change

It is, of course, no guarantee that companies with positive norms operating in all these areas will be successful – they might be making and selling the wrong things at the wrong price to the wrong people – but their chances of getting it right must, all other factors being equal, be considerably greater than those with negative norms.

How to identify norms

The manager who wants to begin to find out what the norm pattern of his organization looks like could do worse than to begin by asking relevant questions and making pertinent observations around those ten areas. Asking questions of subordinates in these areas is fraught with all the well-known pitfalls such as hearing what you want to hear, being told what people think you should hear and of course hitting the first negative norm of 'you don't ask questions like that around here'.

One can use questionnaire methods or independent individuals such as consultants to help but the most valuable instruments of data collection, if used skilfully, are your own eyes, ears and instincts. After all, it is what people *do* in their normal day-to-day behaviour that gives you clues about norms existing in your organization.

Try thinking about your own areas of responsibility, be it the whole company, or a department of it. Ask yourself the following questions and see if it tells you anything about the norms in your system:

* When you ring up the office from outside how do you feel you are treated?

* When did you last engage in some personal or managerial development activity yourself?

* When your staff come to you with ideas or proposals for improvement, are they presented in terms of return on investment or contribution to profitability?

* Are you often surprised by things that you find out? If so, one norm might be 'don't let the boss know'.

* Do you operate, or try to operate, a 'firm and fair' policy with your staff? (This means that norms of 'fairness' will undoubtedly be more important than 'effective performance' on occasions. What could the implications be?)

* What behaviours are rewarded and reinforced in the company? By you? Do you encourage staff to challenge you, for example? How far?

By thinking about the day-to-day running of the business, what people actually do rather than what they are officially supposed to do, a great deal can be found out about the norm pattern of the organization. This should in turn begin to give some clues as to how to tackle any changes needed.

'Feeding' norms – what behaviour is rewarded?

Let us consider the crucial issue of how the norms are reinforced. We can do this by focusing on the last question above, 'What behaviours are rewarded and reinforced in the company (or in my department)?' This is a fascinating, and telling, question if considered honestly. It is my experience that the initial response is very consistent and typical. 'We reward high performance' is the usual response. Excellent answer – it should be given a prize for its 'rightness'. It is what most managers genuinely believe they reward people for – indeed what *they* are rewarded for. This is certainly partly true, but when one begins to dig around, and think a bit more, it is not quite that simple.

Let us examine a hypothetical situation. A manager is given the task of sorting out the performance of a low morale, low productivity area of the company. The goal is clear – to increase output of goods or services by X per cent over X months, and also to improve morale. The previous manager is now in a more senior role elsewhere in the hierarchy and is very keen that mud should not fly in his direction. I suspect the picture is becoming clearer – and is not uncommon in outline. The question now is, if the manager does a good job – a high performance job – but in the process highlights deficiencies which reflect elsewhere in the company hierarchy, what will he be rewarded for doing? Digging out the causes of the problems so that the organization can learn from them, or being more circumspect and leaving stones unturned? In some organizations he will surely feel pressure to behave in ways which will achieve a result without rocking the boat too much.

So, whilst not denying that for most managers high performance is rewarded and encouraged, it is certainly only done so within limits, and those limits are determined not by rational criteria, but by the norms of the submerged organization, your own values and beliefs as a manager, and the way your outlook manifests itself in your behaviour.

Next time you hear yourself saying 'I always keep my door open' or 'I'm always available to my staff', ask yourself 'Why?' or 'How do I encourage them to behave when they come through the door?' or 'Am I encouraging them to rely on me too much?'

For example, an open door policy can encourage your staff to become very dependent upon you by checking everything out. You may, by a raise of the eyebrows, the physical arrangement of your office, your manner, encourage a range of behaviour from downright submission and helplessness to challenge and confrontation. That depends on the very subtle range of signals you give, rather than whether your door is open or not. You create and reinforce a lot of the norms in your patch of the organization, so be aware of your power.

Attempting to find out what your staff *feel* rewarded for is important. It is this which will influence their behaviour, not what you *think* you reward them for.

DIAGNOSING READINESS TO CHANGE

There is a simple rule of thumb you can apply to the likelihood of succeeding in changing a system – whether it be a person or an organization. The forces for change *within* the system as well as *outside* it need to be present and equally strong before movement is likely. Let us take an example from my own experience. I had been considerably overweight for many years. I knew – cognitively – it was bad for me. I was also told regularly by friends and family that they would like me to be thinner. Nothing happened. Why? Because the internal pressures were not sufficient to equal the external pressures and trigger *activity*. Then I suddenly found one day that my health was poor and my doctor related the problem directly to overweight. At the same time I found I could no longer wear my favourite clothes because they were too small! Now the forces were strong both internally and externally and I changed my exercise and eating habits and have lost a considerable amount of weight.

The analogy is transferable to organizational systems. There are many examples where environmental competitive pressures have built up around companies and where top management, at a cognitive level, recognize that things should change. It usually takes some definite internal pressure to build up before action is taken. This can range from workforce disruption to the resignation of key people from the organization. The internal and external forces have to be strongly present in roughly equal proportions before movement will take place.

From the point of view of the manager who wants to act as a catalyst for change, this means working both internally and externally to the system in question to create sufficient unrest with the status quo. An essentially subversive, but necessary, activity.

In a Swedish savings bank the board described ten key learning points that had emerged from a major change they had recently been through. The one which was of particular relevance to this issue was their conviction that 'a catalyst was essential to ask the hard questions which an internal person could not ask and to give the top executives bad feelings about their current behaviour'.

This strikes me as an excellent example of the recognition of the need to convert 'intellectual intentions' into 'gut-felt actions'. This process of moving a system from intention to action is a crucial one.

The 'Felt Security' model

Another way of considering readiness is once again to examine forces in the situation but especially in relation to the degree of *security* that is felt to exist amongst the people in the system undergoing the change.

If we begin by recognizing that there is a scale of *felt security* which is an emotional measure of comfort or threat in a change situation, it follows that this scale can range from low to high. What we can then do is to determine what issues or events are causing the level of security that is felt by individuals or groups in the system. These forces are essentially of two types: forces within individuals; forces in the organization system itself.

Forces in the individual

These forces are already described in some detail at the beginning of this book. They are the range of psychological issues which always come into play when changes are required. They concern feelings about such things as:

— 'Will my knowledge and expertise still be of value?'

— 'Do I feel good about myself?'

— 'How well-motivated am I to perform?'

They also have to do with personality, behaviour and issues such as degree of self-awareness and tolerance of ambiguity. Depending on whether these forces are positive or negative they will lead to a degree of 'felt security' in the individual.

Forces in the organization system

The other set of forces which impinge on feelings of security are those to do with the organization itself. They hinge around such issues as:

— Organization climate or culture – does it encourage or discourage risk-taking?

— Will a department gain or lose status/power in the change?

— What are the perceived consequences of complying or resisting?

— What are the consequences of success or failure?

Again, the answers to these questions will lead to a degree of 'felt security' in the system.

It should now be possible to make a crude assessment of the degree of felt security in the system where change is intended. My experience shows that where a system is experiencing very low or very high felt security the response to change is more likely to be negative. In the case of great insecurity there is a natural tendency to retrench and dig in (rather like the shock phase of reacting to a crisis described earlier). We currently see exactly that situation being acted out by the Fleet Street print unions. They are deeply into defensive retreat. However, there are exceptions. British Leyland under Michael Edwardes was able to force changes in time of extreme insecurity, which otherwise might never have happened. So the type of company and people involved clearly can cause different reactions on occasions. Previous experience of leading 'unstructured' group training sessions (called 'T' groups) in the late 1960s had shown me the same symptoms. When the stress level rose and personal security – normally provided by the structure – was removed, the learning often stopped because participants became rigid and rejected the method. This is why the totally 'unstructured' approach was unsuccessful for a great deal of people. It also has implications for the managers who follow the dictat 'Fear is the best motivator', because the result is usually rigidity and hostility.

Likewise, where security is very high, as in the case of a company which is very successful, or a manager who has always succeeded in the past, it is not always easy to achieve movement due to a heavily filtered perception of reality and a conviction that everything is fine. It is at these ends of the emotional security spectrum that it is most difficult to hear the warning signals and, therefore, the most vulnerable place to be. Again I emphasize that there are organizations where this is not the case, such as universities in the sixties where life was rosy but great strides were made.

Action therefore (in most cases) needs to be taken to move the individual or the system towards the middle of the scale where there is the greatest likelihood of recognizing the need to change and exploring alternatives.

DIAGNOSING READINESS TO CHANGE

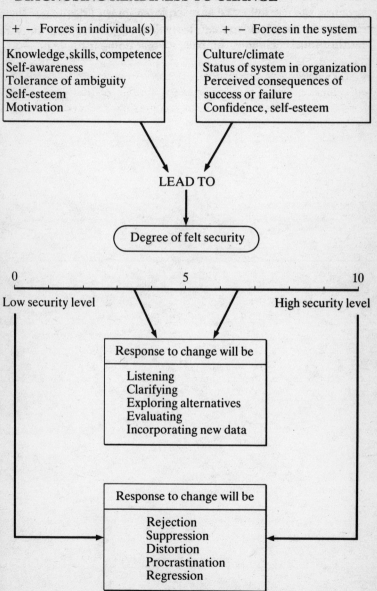

+ – Forces in individual(s)	+ – Forces in the system
Knowledge, skills, competence Self-awareness Tolerance of ambiguity Self-esteem Motivation	Culture/climate Status of system in organization Perceived consequences of success or failure Confidence, self-esteem

LEAD TO

Degree of felt security

0	5	10
Low security level		High security level

Response to change will be

Listening
Clarifying
Exploring alternatives
Evaluating
Incorporating new data

Response to change will be

Rejection
Suppression
Distortion
Procrastination
Regression

Managing Change and Making It Stick

We have now looked at a number of ways of collating and framing data to make it usable. We have explored some of the issues which need to be faced en route. This will be a good opportunity to return to the beginning and have a go at doing it for real.

Good Luck!

SELECT BIBLIOGRAPHY

BENNIS, WARREN G. *Beyond Bureaucracy*, McGraw Hill, New York 1973.

BEYNON, H. *Working for Ford*, London 1984.

BLAKE, AVIS & MOUTON *Corporate Darwinism*, Gulf Publishing, Houston, Texas 1966.

DEAL, TERENCE E. and KENNEDY, ALLAN *Corporate Cultures: Rights and Rituals of Corporate Life*, Addison-Wesley, London 1984.

DRUCKER, P. *The Practice of Management*, Pan Books, London 1968.

—— *Managing in Turbulent Times*, Pan Books, London 1981.

EMERY, F.E. (ed.) *Systems Thinking*, 2nd rev. ed. Penguin Management, London 1981.

GREINER, L.E. 'Evolution and Revolution as Organizations Grow', *Harvard Business Review*, 1972, no. 4, p. 37.

KANTER, ROSABETH MOSS *The Change Masters*, Allen and Unwin, London 1983.

LIEVEGOED, B.C.J. *The Developing Organization*, Tavistock, London 1973.

PETTIGREW, ANDREW *The Awakening Giant*, Blackwell, Oxford 1985.

The Association for Management Education and Development is the only voluntary association of professionals in the UK whose work focuses exclusively on management training, education and organization development. Membership is open to anyone involved in this significant field of work. The Association's fast growth in recent years has created a lively membership of interested people in business, government, voluntary organization, academic institutions and management consultancy.

The main aim of the Association for Management Education and Development is to promote high standards of management performance so that people in organizations and communities can work with greater effectiveness. Members are therefore encouraged to meet and collaborate to improve their own professional capabilities. Activities include evening and one-day meetings, and three- to four-day events held all over the UK and in Europe. These are designed to provide members with different developmental opportunities for the various stages of their careers. They also enable members to extend their knowledge and skills, to keep in touch with frontier thinking on management, and to exchange ideas and experience.

Free publications are sent to members. These include *MEAD* (Management Education and Development), a journal which has three issues a year and contains articles on current management training and development; frequent focus papers on topical issues; and a monthly newsletter.

For further information, contact:

The Association for Management Education and Development
Polytechnic of Central London
35 Marylebone Road
London
NW1 5LS

01-486 5811 (ex. 259)